POCKET FACTFILES

Birds

Project Director: **Graham Bateman**
Managing Editor: **Shaun Barrington**
Picture Manager: **Claire Turner**
Production: **Clive Sparling**
Cartography: **Tim Williams**
Design & Editorial: **Kinsey & Harrison**
  Designer: **Edward Kinsey**
  Editors: **James Harrison,**
        Louisa Somerville

Produced by
Andromeda Oxford Limited,
Kimber House, 1 Kimber Road
Abingdon, Oxfordshire OX14 1BZ
www.andromeda.co.uk

Library of Congress Cataloging-in-
Publication Data Available

10 9 8 7 6 5 4 3 2 1

Published in 2003 by Sterling Publishing
Co., Inc.
387 Park Avenue South,
New York, NY 10016
Distributed in Canada by Sterling
Publishing,
c/o Manda Group,
One Atlantic Avenue, Suite 105
Toronto, Ontario, Canada M6K 3E7

Printed in Hong Kong

Sterling ISBN 1-4027-0294-9

Photographic Credits

Ardea Jim Zipp 100–101; Graeme Chapman 207;
Dennis Avon 213

Nature Picture Library Steve Knell 157

Oxford Scientific Films Jorge Sierra Antinolo
17; Tui De Roy 19, 229; C.M. Perrins 21; Mark
Hamblin 30–31, 45, 58, 67, 73, 187; Eyal Bartov
32–33; Konrad Wothe 37, 123; Patti Murray/
Animals Animals 41; David & Sue Cayless 43;
Michael Sewell/Visual Pursuit 51; Stan Osolinski
55; Tom Leach 63; Carlos Sanchez Alonso 65;
Peter Hawkey/Survival Anglia 71; Mark Jones
79; Tom Ulrich 87, 132, 231; John Downer 93;
Dennis Green/Survival Anglia Limited 111; Jen &
Des Bartlett/Survival Anglia 120–121, 126–127;
David Tipling 131; David Cayless 143; Adrian
Bailey 145; Daybreak Imagery 179, 201, 243;
Niall Benvie 185, 209; Tony Tilford 211; David M.
Cottridge 223; Steve Littlewood 237; Michael
Fogden 245

Tim Laman 249

All artwork copyright Andromeda Oxford Ltd.

POCKET FACTFILES
Birds

Sterling Publishing Co., Inc.
New York

CONTENTS

LARGE GROUND BIRDS 120

SONGBIRDS 148

GLOSSARY 250 INDEX 254

INTRODUCTION

OF ALL THE VERTEBRATES, BIRDS are the most noticeable. Whereas most mammals, reptiles, and amphibians are secretive, well camouflaged or nocturnal, and fish live in a separate, underwater world, birds are all around us, and many of them have bright plumage as well as distinctive calls and songs. Unlike almost all fish, amphibians, and reptiles, but like mammals, birds are warm-blooded (the scientific term is endothermic).

Although bats among the mammals and many insects can fly, it is the birds that have mastered the ability of flight to the greatest degree. Crucial to this is their evolution of feathers, which are unique to birds. Some birds, such as the swift (*see page 104*) and the albatross (*see page 18*) spend virtually all their life on the wing. Furthermore, the bird's entire basic body plan is adapted for flight. The skeleton is amazingly lightweight yet strong, with many of the bones reduced in size, honeycombed with air spaces between supporting struts, or fused to produce a rigid framework. The forelimbs are modified into wings, powered by big flight muscles, while the bony tail has become a fan of feathers that helps the bird steer in flight. Instead of having heavy jaws, the bird's mandibles are modified to

TAKING OFF AND LANDING
Take off is achieved by a jump into the air and keeping the angle of the body at 45°. In landing, the wings tilt the body almost vertically.

form a lightweight but powerful bill (or beak) with a tough horny covering. Bills come in an amazing variety of shapes related to each species' diet and feeding methods: the long, delicate bills of hummingbirds are designed for drinking nectar from deep within flowers while the strange, upside-down bills of flamingos, with their complex internal structure, filter out tiny organisms from water. In contrast to almost all mammals, birds reproduce by laying big, yolk-rich eggs, so avoiding carrying round a heavy embryo within the body, which would prevent them flying.

There is no doubt that birds are a highly successful and varied group of animals: with almost 10,000 species, they can boast more diversity than any other class of vertebrates, apart from the ray-finned fishes (which include over 24,000, and probably many more, species). This is well over twice the number of species of mammals, for instance. Their powers of flight have enabled birds to travel far across the globe to exploit new opportunities. Although many birds are resident year-round in the same region, others make epic annual journeys between breeding grounds and wintering grounds. They include the world's greatest migrant, the Arctic tern (*see page 70*), which travels between the north and south poles every year of its life.

THE BIRDS IN THIS BOOK

In *Pocket Factfile: Birds*, examples have been selected from the major groups of birds to highlight the extraordinary diversity of their structure, habitat, and lifestyle. The selection gives an idea of the many remarkable adaptations that various species have evolved to help them survive, from the lammergeier's habit of dropping bones onto rocks to shatter them so that it can eat the splinters and the rich marrow within (*see page 80*), to that of the northern mockingbird (*see page 170*) and superb lyrebird (*see page 152*), which can mimic the voices of many other bird species as well as a whole range of other sounds, from a barking dog to a chainsaw.

The birds in this book include familiar, common and widespread species, such as the house sparrow (*see page 214*), and rare, threatened and very localized ones, such as the whooping crane (*see page 50*), which is found in only a few places in very small numbers. The choice of species also reflects the wide range of diets and feeding methods found in different groups of birds. Some are extremely specialist, for example the snail kite (*see page 86*), which feeds almost entirely on just one kind of freshwater snail.

In size, the birds in this book range from the tiny hummingbirds, the world's smallest birds, including the ruby-throated hummingbird (*see page 242*), through to small and medium-sized types such as perching birds, to the birds of prey such as the bald eagle (*see page 90*), and huge birds like the Andean condor (*see page 78*) and biggest of them all, the flightless ostrich (*page 120*), emu (*page 126*) and relatives.

BIRD CLASSIFICATION

Like other animals, birds are classified scientifically according to a strict hierarchical system. The basic unit is the species. Similar species are grouped together in genera (singular genus), similar genera into families (ending in -idae), and families into orders (ending in -iformes). The names of each level are Latinized words.

Although this may seem complicated, the system is very logical and scientific names have the great advantage of being recognized worldwide, unlike common names. Each species has a unique, two-part name. The first part is the name of the genus to which the species belongs, for example, *Ramphastos*, used for all the larger species of toucans. The second part denotes the species, for instance, *toco*, identifying its owner as the toco toucan. All toucans are classified in a single family, Ramphastidae, which are grouped with woodpeckers and other related birds in the order Piciformes.

IN FLIGHT
Flight and covert feathers give lift for flight, while contour feathers provide warmth and aerodynamic shape.

UPPER WING SURFACE

Lesser coverts
Secondary flight feathers
Greater coverts
Primary flight feathers
Secondary coverts

LOWER WING SURFACE

Secondary flight feathers
Primary flight feathers

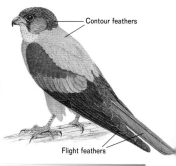

Contour feathers
Flight feathers

EMPEROR PENGUIN

Aptenodytes forsteri
Family: SPHENISCIDAE
Order: SPHENISCIFORMES

DISTRIBUTION: Southern Ocean around Antarctica and the sub-Antarctic; breeds on sea ice or farther inland.

SIZE: Length 44–45in (112–115cm); weight 50–100lb (22.7–45.3kg).

APPEARANCE: Very large penguin. Black head and back; white breast and undersides of wings; distinctive orange-yellow patch on each side of neck, fading to yellow on throat. Black feet; black bill with pink or lilac streak on lower mandible; eyes normally dark brown.

DIET: Mainly fish, plus squid and krill. Captures prey by pursuing it underwater.

BREEDING: Breeds in large colonies in winter, mainly on sea ice. Does not build a nest. Male incubates single egg on his feet beneath a fold of skin until it hatches after 60–66 days. Female then returns from sea and takes over to brood chick and feed it on regurgitated fish, while male goes to sea to feed. After about 45 days, young penguins join a crèche. They fledge at 5 months.

LIFESTYLE: The emperor is the biggest of the penguins, and the heaviest of all seabirds. Its bulk, and its thick fat layers and dense plumage, help it conserve heat in the bitter Antarctic winter, enabling it to survive the coldest climate on Earth. It is rarely seen north of the sea ice that surrounds Antarctica.

Emperor penguins often catch krill swarming beneath ice floes, but their main prey are fish. Propelling themselves with their flipper-like wings, they chase fish and catch them one by one. They may dive to depths of 650 feet (200m) or more in pursuit of prey, and have even been recorded 1,750 feet (534m) below the surface – deep in the twilight zone of the ocean, and far deeper than any other diving bird.

DEVOTED PARENT
Despite his starved state the male emperor gives his newly hatched chick a meal of milk-like fluid from his gullet, before the female returns with a crop full of fish.

Although most emperor penguins breed on sea ice, the breeding sites are often far from open water. The birds may have to walk 125 miles (200km) to reach them, making short incubation shifts impossible. So once the female has laid her single egg, she goes to sea while the male does all the incubation, in winter temperatures that sink as low as -15°F (-60°C). The males huddle together for warmth, but since they cannot go to sea to feed they lose up to 45 percent of their body weight over a period of 110 days. The females return just as the chicks hatch, and the starved males are able to head for open water for a well-earned meal.

JACKASS PENGUIN

> *Spheniscus demersus*
> Family: SPHENISCIDAE
> Order: SPHENISCIFORMES

DISTRIBUTION: Seas off coasts of South Africa and Namibia, coming ashore to breed, rest and molt, currently mainly on 24 inshore islands, also at 3 coastal sites.

SIZE: Length 24–27.5in (60–70cm); weight 4.4–8.8lb (2–4kg).

APPEARANCE: Medium-sized penguin with strong blade-shaped bill (slightly larger, deeper in male). Black on back, head and wings, with white on belly extending up in a narrowing band onto head, as far as base of bill; black horseshoe on breast, extending down flanks to thighs; variable amount of black spots on breast and belly; white patches on underwings; legs and bill black, with pale gray band near tip; eyes dark brown. Juvenile dark grayish-blue at first, turning browner; develops face pattern in second and third year.

DIET: Feeds in inshore waters, mainly on small shoaling fish; also eats some crustaceans and squid.

BREEDING: Females may lay eggs at any time of year, though there are two peaks of egg-laying, in February-May and November-December. Breed in colonies, making nests in burrows, under rocks or bushes, or on ground, of seaweed and guano, stones. 2, rarely 1, chalky white eggs, incubated by both parents for 38–41 days. Young may join small crèches in surface-nesting colonies. Fledge at 64–110 days.

LIFESTYLE: Also known as the African penguin, the jackass penguin is so-called because of its loud calls, like the braying of an ass. With variations, these sounds serve as display calls by males advertising nest sites to prospective mates, as well as being made by both sexes during pair-bonding rituals.

Jackass penguins spend much of their lives in small groups at sea, usually within 25 miles (40km) of the shore. Here, they dive to chase and catch their prey, generally reaching 100–300 feet (30–90m) below the surface. Most feeding groups leave the colony on shore around dawn, returning in the late afternoon or early evening, though some remain at sea overnight.

Jackass penguins have suffered a rapid population decline, due mainly to people taking their eggs on a large scale, damaging their breeding habitat as a result of collecting their droppings (guano) for use as a fertilizer, and reducing numbers of their prey by over-fishing. A major oilspill in 2000 affected over 40 percent of the total population, but many were saved during the world's biggest seabird rescue operation.

PROTECTED SPECIES
Today, laws protect South African jackass penguin breeding colonies from damage through egg collection and guano collection. But sharks, gulls, and feral cats remain serious predators.

RED-THROATED LOON

Gavia stellata
Family: GAVIIDAE
Order: GAVIIFORMES

DISTRIBUTION: Breeds on tundra and moorland all around the Arctic and sub-Arctic, mainly on lakes. Winters farther south in coastal waters, sometimes on lakes.

SIZE: Length 21–27in (53–69cm); weight 2.5–4.4lb (1.15–1.98kg).

APPEARANCE: Sleek, graceful bird with long, sharp bill. Breeding plumage uniformly grayish-brown on upperparts, with dark rust-red throat patch and vertical black-and-white stripes from nape of neck to crown; white underparts. Legs dark gray; bill paler gray; eyes reddish-brown. In winter loses red throat; gray back finely spotted white. Sexes similar.

DIET: Mainly fish; also frogs, crustaceans, and mollusks.

BREEDING: May to June. Nest ranges from simple scrape to heap of vegetation in shallow water. Lays 2 olive eggs, with brown blotches. Eggs incubated by both parents (but mainly female) for 24–29 days. Chicks leave nest and can swim soon after hatching, but usually stay under parent's wing or on its back; fledge at 2 months.

LIFESTYLE: The slender, elegant red-throated loon is the smallest of the loons or divers: a small family of just four large waterbirds that are highly adapted for hunting fish and other prey underwater. Its lower body weight allows it to take off without a long run across the water, unlike its larger relatives, and this allows it to nest beside much smaller lakes and pools on its bleak northern breeding grounds. But such waters rarely provide enough fish to support a pair of loons and their young, and the adult birds have to make regular trips to larger lakes to find food.

It hunts its prey underwater, using its powerful webbed feet to drive itself through the water while it keeps its wings folded tight to its

TIPPING THE BALANCE
The red-throated loon's legs are set well back on its body for efficiency when swimming. But this makes them almost useless on dry land, and the loon cannot walk properly.

streamlined body. It can adjust its buoyancy like a submarine, by regulating the amount of air in its lungs and associated air sacs. It hunts by sight, and may stay underwater for several minutes.

Although the female lays two eggs, one chick often dies because a stronger chick monopolizes the food brought by the parents. Loons may also suffer from poisoning by pesticides or oil pollution, but these dangers are not such a problem in the far north where they breed.

GREAT CRESTED GREBE

Podiceps cristatus
Family: PODICIPEDIDAE
Order: PODICIPEDIFORMES

DISTRIBUTION: There are three main populations: a northern group, breeding by fresh or brackish lakes and ponds or slow rivers from northern Europe to China, wintering off coasts farther south; scattered populations in Africa; (most in the south) and another in Australia and New Zealand.

SIZE: Length 18–20in (46–51cm); weight 1.3–3.3lb (0.6–1.5kg).

APPEARANCE: A slim, long-necked waterbird with a flat head, crimson eyes, pinkish bill, and greenish legs. Breeding plumage dark brown with black double-horned crest on head, white face with chestnut and black frill, white foreneck and breast. Non-breeding adult paler.

DIET: Mainly small fish, but also aquatic insects and their larvae, crawfish, shrimps, and other crustaceans, snails and other mollusks, and amphibians. Pursues swimming prey underwater. Feeds insects and spiders to young.

BREEDING: Usually in spring in temperate climates, nonseasonal in tropics. Builds a nest platform of rotting vegetation at edge of water, sometimes floating. 3–6 white eggs, incubated by both parents for 25–31 days. Chicks fledge at 71–79 days. Sometimes rears 2 broods a year.

LIFESTYLE: The elegant, sharp-billed great crested grebe is an expert diver that takes most of its prey underwater, slipping smoothly beneath the surface and chasing fish with powerful strokes of its webbed feet. On the surface it swims with its body low in the water and its neck upright. Like other grebes it needs a lengthy take-off, pattering its feet over the water and taking to the air with fast, rather labored wingbeats. Once in the air it flies with its feet trailing and its long, extended neck held low,

giving it an oddly hump-backed appearance. In early spring the adult grebes engage in dramatic courtship rituals involving flamboyant displays, graceful necking, and the "penguin dance" which involves a courting pair paddling furiously to rise upright from the water. Breast to breast, their bills full of waterweed, they shake their heads from side to side in a ceremonial display before subsiding back into the water.

ELEGANT DIVER
Strictly aquatic, the great crested grebe may even nest on a raft of vegetation (*above*). In spring its courtship displays show off its plumage to spectacular effect (*right*).

ROYAL ALBATROSS

Diomedea epomophora
Family: DIOMEDEIDAE
Order: PROCELLARIIFORMES

DISTRIBUTION: Breeds around New Zealand, on Campbell Island, Auckland Islands and Chatham Islands, with a very small colony on the Otago Peninsula, South Island, New Zealand. Disperses widely over Southern Ocean after breeding, when most commonly recorded off New Zealand and South America.

SIZE: Length 42–48in (107–122cm); weight 14-23lb (6.5–10.3kg).

APPEARANCE: A huge seabird, with a white head, body, and tail. Many researchers separate the royal albatross into distinct northern and southern species; upperwings of northern royal albatross all-black, those of southern species white with black flight feathers, underwings of both white with black trailing edges and wingtips; bill long, flesh-colored with yellowish hooked tip and black cutting edges, legs and feet pinkish-gray. Juveniles have dark flecks on back and tail.

DIET: Mainly squid; also some fish, crustaceans, and salps (translucent relatives of sea-squirts).

BREEDING: Every other year, in spring, if chick is successfully reared. Nest a mound of vegetation on the ground, surrounded by a rim of mud or a ditch. Colonial; pairs nest far apart or closer together, depending on circumstances. 1 whitish egg, incubated by both parents for 74–85 days. Chicks brooded for 21–43 days; fledge after 216-257 days. Reach sexual maturity at 6–22 years.

LIFESTYLE: With a wingspan of up to 10.6 feet (3.2m) or more, the royal albatross is a superb flier, traveling hundreds of miles each day in its search for food, with scarcely a wingbeat and minimal expenditure of energy.

As they can live up to 55 years or more , and breed only very slowly, royal albatrosses are extremely

vulnerable to population declines. Human visitors to their breeding colonies, as well as the mammals they brought with them, have wiped out huge numbers, and pigs and cats and stoats still take eggs and chicks. Storm damage on the Chatham Islands removed soil and vegetation, hugely reducing breeding success. Many birds are caught and drowned on hooks set from long-lining fishing boats.

ENERGY SAVER
Like other albatrosses, the royal has a tendon mechanism in its shoulders that locks the wings and prevents them moving above the horizontal when gliding, so saving energy.

NORTHERN FULMAR

Fulmarus glacialis
Family: PROCELLARIIDAE
Order: PROCELLARIIFORMES

DISTRIBUTION: Breeds on rocky coasts and islands across much of the Arctic, north Atlantic, and north Pacific regions. Northernmost birds migrate south to feed in ice-free ocean waters, while those further south disperse out to sea.

SIZE: Length 18–20in (45–50cm); weight 1.5–2lb (0.7–0.9kg)

APPEARANCE: Stout-bodied, with thick neck; stubby, hooked yellow bill with prominent tubular nostrils on top; short, diamond-shaped tail and stiff wings. Most fulmars have gray and white plumage, like that of gulls, but many Arctic birds are darker overall.

DIET: Fish, small squid, jellyfish, crustaceans, and other oceanic creatures; also fish offal jettisoned from ships.

BREEDING: Nests in coastal cliff colonies each spring, but may claim territory well before breeding. Lays 1 white egg on bare rock ledge or hollow; incubation 47–53 days, by both sexes; young fledge after 46–53 days. Breeds for first time at the age of 7–10 years.

LIFESTYLE: Although it looks like a gull, the northern fulmar is really a tubenosed petrel: a relative of the great albatrosses that patrol the storm-driven waves of the southern oceans. It flies like a miniature albatross, gliding and soaring on stiff, straight wings. It copes superbly with high winds, rolling and tilting through the wave troughs in long, confident glides, and riding the updrafts around sheer cliffs with effortless grace.

Northern fulmars spend most of their lives feeding at sea, far from land. They often rest on the water, swimming buoyantly like ducks. Their legs are well adapted for swimming but almost useless on land, and fulmars visit the land only to breed, on coastal sites such as cliffs with easy access by air.

Fulmar pairs prefer to lay on narrow ledges near the tops of cliffs, where soil or grass provides a cushion for their single egg. Once they have bred successfully they return to the same nest sites and mates each year, often in the fall before the spring breeding season. The pairs greet each other and defend their nest sites against neighbors with raucous cackling calls, and head-waving, bowing displays. When the single chick hatches, its parents feed it on a concentrated "soup" of partly digested fish and fish oil.

Northern fulmars have flourished over the last century, specially in the north Atlantic. Their success may be linked to their habit of following fishing boats and feasting on fish offal discarded after the catch is processed. There are many more such boats than there used to be, and northern fulmars seem to be reaping the benefit.

SMELLY DEFENSE
A northern fulmar defends its single egg or chick by spitting foul-smelling fish oil at anything – or anyone – who gets too close to its narrow nesting ledge on a coastal cliff.

GREAT WHITE PELICAN

Pelecanus onocrotalus
Family: PELECANIDAE
Order: PELECANIFORMES

DISTRIBUTION: Lakes and inland seas in southeastern Europe, Turkey, west-central Asia, northern India, and throughout much of Africa. Northern birds migrate south for the winter.

SIZE: Length 55–69in (140–175cm); weight up to 24lb (11kg).

APPEARANCE: Huge, long-necked waterbird with very short tail, and long pinkish bill with large yellow pouch extending from throat to near tip of lower mandible. Plumage mainly white, with outer primary feathers black above, and all primaries black below. Pink legs and feet with all four toes webbed. Red eyes.

DIET: Fish, caught by dipping bill underwater with pouch held open to form a scoop. Often fishes in cooperative groups.

BREEDING: In spring in north of range, in large, dense colonies. Some colonies may contain up to 40,000 breeding pairs. Each pair builds a large pile of reeds, twigs and other plant material, usually in a reedbed or on an island in dense wetland vegetation, but sometimes on bare soil or rock far from water. 1–3 chalky white eggs, incubated for 35–36 days. Chicks fledge in 65–70 days.

LIFESTYLE: The great white pelican is an extremely sociable bird that breeds, roosts, and feeds in spectacular flocks of from 50 to 500 birds. The flocks are often nomadic outside the breeding season, traveling between feeding grounds. Groups of pelicans fish cooperatively, swimming forward in a semicircle to herd the fish together. Each bird uses its great bill pouch like a fishing net, rapidly plunging its bill below the surface and opening the pouch to scoop up an immense weight of fish and water. It then drains off the water before swallowing the fish whole. It eats about 2.5lb (1.2kg) of fish a day – either many small ones or a few large ones – and contrary to common belief it never carries fish in its pouch.

In the breeding season an adult pelican develops a short crest, a pinkish bloom on its plumage, a yellow breast patch, and a colored patch of bare skin on its forehead – pinkish yellow in males, but orange in females. The males display in groups to attract receptive females, but during disputes over the same female a dominant male threatens any rivals to drive them away. Once the pairs have formed they nest in close company, often touching each other.

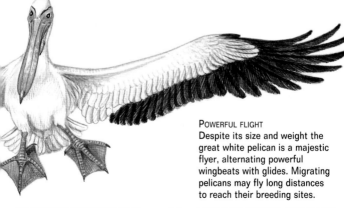

POWERFUL FLIGHT
Despite its size and weight the great white pelican is a majestic flyer, alternating powerful wingbeats with glides. Migrating pelicans may fly long distances to reach their breeding sites.

GREAT FRIGATEBIRD

Fregata minor
Family: FREGATIDAE
Order: PELECANIFORMES

DISTRIBUTION: Widespread in tropical and subtropical Indian and Pacific Oceans, and off Brazil in the Atlantic. Breeds on oceanic islands and along coasts.

SIZE: Length 34–39in (86–100cm); weight 1.4–3.4lb (0.6–1.5kg).

APPEARANCE: Large seabird with long, narrow wings, deeply forked tail, and long, hooked bill. Male black with green sheen, pale brown wingbar, scarlet throat and feet. Female mainly dark brown, and usually larger than male.

DIET: Mainly fish, especially flying-fish; also young birds. Feeds on the wing by snatching prey from surface waters, or seizing flying-fish in mid-air. Often obtains food by harassing other flying birds and stealing their prey.

BREEDING: In trees and bushes on island colonies, often with other seabirds, every two years. Single white egg, incubated in twig nest by both parents for 40–50 days. Young hatches naked; fledges at 6 months, but relies on its parents for 6 more months.

LIFESTYLE: Although it cannot swim, and can only get back in the air with difficulty if it lands in the water, the great frigatebird spends most of life far from land, soaring and gliding over the ocean. It has a wingspan of over 6 feet (1.8m) but weighs very little; this enables it to ride the ocean winds with barely a wingbeat, staying aloft for hours on end before returning to land to roost for the night.

COLORFUL DRUM
Inflated with air, the scarlet throat pouch of the male great frigatebird acts as a resonator, producing a loud, low drumming note as he rattles his bill against it during his courtship display.

Out at sea it feeds mainly on fish and squid swimming at the surface, and often follows schools of predatory tuna or dolphins so it can seize fish that they scare to the surface. Thanks to its long bill it usually manages to snatch its prey without getting its feathers wet – a vital consideration for a bird that does not have waterproof plumage. Its favorite victims are flying-fish, which it can catch in mid-air.

At its island breeding colonies the frigatebird gets a lot of its food by piracy. It chases other seabirds as they return with their crops full of fish, and scares them into disgorging their catch. If a victim resists, the pirate may even attack it in the air by pulling on a wing feather to knock it off balance. When the luckless bird finally gives in and drops its catch, the pirate swoops down to snatch it as it falls.

The males gather to attract females by a communal treetop display. Spreading and fluttering their long wings, they throw back their heads to reveal their inflated, scarlet throat pouches while calling and rattling their bills. When a female has chosen a male from the group, she builds a nest with material gathered – and often stolen from neighbors – by the male. Rearing the single chick takes so long that the birds can breed only once every two years.

CAPE GANNET

Morus capensis
Family: SULIDAE
Order: PELECANIFORMES

DISTRIBUTION: Breeds along coasts of South Africa and Namibia. Winters on both coasts of African mainland, north to Gulf of Guinea on west coast and Mozambique on east coast.

SIZE: Length 33–37in (84–94cm); weight 5.7lb (2.6kg).

APPEARANCE: Large black-and-white seabird with yellow head and nape, and a long black stripe down center of throat. Juveniles are all brown, speckled paler; as they grow, they pass through various checkered stages with increasing amounts of white in the plumage. Bill powerful and pointed, with fine serrations near tip. Feet large, with webs between all four toes.

DIET: Mainly shoaling fish in surface waters, particularly anchovies, sardines and saury; also offal discarded by fishing boats.

BREEDING: September to April, usually on offshore islands, in large colonies. Nest a mound of debris, cemented together with the birds' droppings. Single blue egg, with chalky white coating, incubated by both parents for 43 to 44 days. Parents place the egg under their feet where it is warmed by the webs, which are rich in blood vessels. To withstand the adult's weight, eggs have very thick shells. Chick fledges at about 3 months.

LIFESTYLE: Cape gannets are very gregarious, feeding and breeding in large groups. The mainly dazzlingly white plumage helps birds from a colony spot other gannets that have found a rich feeding site, so they can all take advantage.

A group of gannets fishing is a thrilling sight, as the birds rain down in all directions from heights of 65 feet (20m) or more like white arrowheads, crisscrossing one another's paths but managing to avoid hitting one another. Their momentum carries them below the

SHOCK ABSORBER
All gannets fold back their wings for stream-lining as they dive for fish; the North Atlantic gannet (*Morus bassanus*) is shown below. Air sacs under the skin of the face cushion the head against the impact.

surface, where they seize a bewildered fish from a shoal in their daggerlike bills and may swallow it underwater, though they often wait until they return to the surface just a few seconds later. At their crowded island breeding colonies, the Cape gannets produce huge amounts of droppings. The hot, arid climate quickly dries them out to produce thick phosphate-rich deposits called guano, harvested by humans for over 170 years for use as an agricultural fertilizer. Overfishing of sardines off the coast of Namibia, have caused a huge gannet decline there.

GREAT CORMORANT

Phalacrocorax carbo
Family: PHALACROCORACIDAE
Order: PELECANIFORMES

DISTRIBUTION: Scattered over large stretches of inland and coastal water, across eastern North America, Europe, Asia, Africa, Australia, and New Zealand.

SIZE: Length 31.5–39in (80–100cm); weight 3.7–5.9lb (1.7–2.7kg).

APPEARANCE: Long-necked diving bird with long, thick, hooked bill, and short wings; black feet have all four toes webbed. Plumage glossy blue-black, with bronze sheen on upper parts, and black-edged wing feathers. White chin, and small yellow throat pouch bordered with white. Develops white flank patches in breeding season.

DIET: Mainly fish, plus squid, crabs, and other aquatic animals. Hunts by diving from surface to pursue prey underwater.

BREEDING: Nests in spring to summer, in large colonies on rocks and cliff ledges, or in trees inland.

The nest is a large, rough cup of seaweed and debris, lined with finer material. 3–4 chalky-blue eggs, incubated under webs of parent's feet for 27–29 days. Chicks fledge after 2 months, but need to be fed by parents for some time after fledging.

FISH THIEF?
Often accused of catching more than its share of fish, the great cormorant is regarded as a pest by many fishermen and has suffered persecution in some parts of its range.

LIFESTYLE: Although it is usually considered a seabird, the great cormorant is very adaptable and often lives far inland, near rivers and lakes. It hunts fish by underwater pursuit, folding its wings and driving itself along with its powerful webbed feet. To make this easier its plumage is not waterproof, so when it dives the air beneath its feathers is displaced and it becomes less buoyant. At the end of a diving session it usually perches on a rock or timber pile with its wings spread to dry.

GRAY HERON

Ardea cinerea
Family: ARDEIDAE
Order: CICONIIFORMES

DISTRIBUTION: Near shallow fresh and brackish water across much of Europe and Asia, from the British Isles to Japan and south to Java; also found in parts of Africa.

SIZE: Length 35–38in (90–98cm); weight 3.5–4.4lb (1.6–2 kg).

APPEARANCE: Tall, long-necked, long-legged wading bird with long, sharp, heavy bill. Gray with white head and neck; black streaks on neck; black eyestripe, extending into black plumes on nape. Black underwings. Bill and bare skin of face yellow-green, becoming pink or orange in breeding season; yellow-brown legs.

DIET: Fish, frogs, small mammals; also crustaceans, aquatic insects, mollusks; sometimes young birds.

BREEDING: In spring in temperate regions, almost all year round in the tropics. Breeds in colonies of up to 1,000 birds in trees, bushes or on cliffs, up to 80 feet (25m) above the ground. Large, untidy stick nest. 3–5 dull, bluish-green eggs, incubated by both parents for 24–25 days. Young birds fledge at 8 weeks.

LIFESTYLE: The gray heron is a widespread, common wading bird, often to be seen standing patiently at the water's edge, watching for prey. It favors the shallow waters of lakes, rivers, and estuaries, where it usually hunts alone for fish, frogs, and other animals. It may stand motionless for long periods, its long neck hunched into its shoulders. When it detects a possible meal it typically tilts forward, extends its head, and stalks through the water with slow, deliberate movements before stabbing down with its long dagger bill. It often catches large eels and flatfish – sometimes so large that it has difficulty swallowing them. If alarmed it takes to the air with

powerful flaps of its very broad
wings and a harsh, croaking call,
descending in a glide or spiraling
aerobatics to land at a safe
distance. Despite its size it moves
with great agility around its treetop
nesting colonies, where the males
perform sky-pointing courtship
displays while clattering their bills
and calling loudly.

RETRACTED HEAD
The gray heron nearly
always flies with its head
retracted over its hunched
neck, and its long legs
extended behind. Its flight is
heavy and ponderous, but it
often soars high in the air.

31

LITTLE EGRET

Egretta garzetta
Family: ARDEIDAE
Order: CICONIIFORMES

DISTRIBUTION: Breeds near rivers, estuaries, lakes, lagoons, and coasts, from southern England to Mediterranean Europe and much of Africa, and east to southern Asia, Japan, and Australia.

SIZE: Length 21–25in (53–64cm); weight 12–21oz (350–550g).

APPEARANCE: Small white heron with a long, slender, sinuous neck, and a long black bill; long black legs with yellow feet. A breeding adult has long, thin, white plumes sprouting from its nape and back.

DIET: Mainly small fish, frogs, and the adults and larvae of insects, plus crustaceans, worms, snails, lizards, and small mammals.

BREEDING: Breeds in spring, nesting in colonies in waterside trees, bushes, and reedbeds, often alongside other herons. 3–6 oval, green-blue eggs, incubated by both parents for 21–22 days. Chicks fledge at 40–45 days.

LIFESTYLE: Lively yet elegant, the little egret typically feeds in shallow water, wading to belly depth and often running about to flush fish and other animals out of hiding. It then seizes them in its long, sharp bill and swallows them whole. It often perches precariously on mats of floating weed, keeping its balance by flapping its half-open

wings. If alarmed it gives a nasal croak and flies off with quite rapid flaps of its bowed wings, holding its head up on its curved neck in typical heron fashion and trailing its conspicuous yellow feet behind it.

Single males advertise for females with short flapping display flights, accompanied by thudding sounds from their wings. Mated pairs greet each other at the nest with a ceremonial display, raising their long plumes and then rattling their bills as they settle back and relax. Colonies are noisy places, as neighboring pairs defend their small territories with quacking, snarling, and croaking calls.

The nuptial plumes of the little egret were once highly valued as adornments for women's hats. Millions of egrets were killed for their plumes in the 1800s and early 1900s, until active campaigning by the early bird protection societies (and changing fashions) removed the threat to its future in the 1920s.

STALKING THE SHALLOWS
Shallow coastal waters can offer rich pickings for little egrets. Although they gather in loose flocks to make the most of a local wealth of prey, they also hunt alone.

AMERICAN BITTERN

Botaurus lentiginosus
Family: ARDEIDAE
Order: CICONIIFORMES

DISTRIBUTION: For nesting, prefers marshes and bogs, inland and on coasts, that have dense vegetation cover, particularly of bulrushes and catstails; on migration and in winter, may turn up in a wider range of habitats, especially freshwater sawgrass and catstail swamps. Breeds from central Canada south through the United States as far as central California, Kansas, and Virginia; northern populations winter south to Panama and the Caribbean.

SIZE: Length 22–33in (56–85cm); weight 13–20oz (370–570g)

APPEARANCE: Large, stocky-bodied, with thicker neck than herons; smallest of the world's four large bitterns; plumage brown, with fine streaks and spots; bold black patch on neck (lacking in juveniles); olive streak of bare skin at base of long daggerlike yellow bill; eyes yellow, legs greenish; underparts streaked brown and white; when it flies, shows blackish flight feathers.

DIET: Mainly fish of a range of species, including catfish, eels, sticklebacks and perch; also a wide variety of other prey at times, ranging from insects, mollusks and crayfish to frogs, salamanders, snakes and small mammals.

BREEDING: Spring and summer; nest a platform of bulrushes or catstails among dense cover, built up on the water or lodged in the vegetation just above it, sometimes on ground; usually 4–5 brownish to olive-buff eggs, incubated by female for 28–29 days; young leave the nest when they are about two weeks old.

LIFESTYLE: The American bittern is active mainly at dusk and during the night. It leads a largely solitary life, standing quietly or slowly stalking its prey in the densely vegetated wetlands it favors. Unlike other bitterns, the American bittern may also breed in open

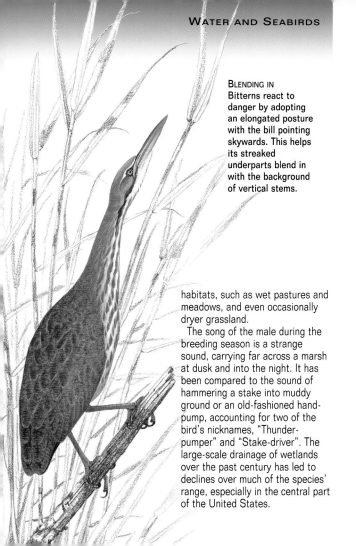

BLENDING IN
Bitterns react to danger by adopting an elongated posture with the bill pointing skywards. This helps its streaked underparts blend in with the background of vertical stems.

habitats, such as wet pastures and meadows, and even occasionally dryer grassland.

The song of the male during the breeding season is a strange sound, carrying far across a marsh at dusk and into the night. It has been compared to the sound of hammering a stake into muddy ground or an old-fashioned hand-pump, accounting for two of the bird's nicknames, "Thunder-pumper" and "Stake-driver". The large-scale drainage of wetlands over the past century has led to declines over much of the species' range, especially in the central part of the United States.

WHITE STORK

Ciconia ciconia
Family: CICONIIDAE
Order: CICONIIFORMES

DISTRIBUTION: Breeds in marshes and on farmland in Iberia, northern Africa, and central Europe north and east to the Baltic countries and southwest Russia; also Asia Minor, south and east Asia. European storks winter in Africa; Asian storks winter in India and south Asia.

SIZE: Length 39–45in (100–115cm); weight 5–9.7lb (2.27–4.40kg).

APPEARANCE: Large white stork with long red bill and red legs; back part of wings black both above and below.

DIET: Frogs, small fish, worms, snails, beetles, and other small invertebrates; sometimes eggs and small mammals.

BREEDING: In spring and summer. Builds large, untidy nest of sticks, lined with grasses and twigs, in trees, on cliff ledges and buildings. 3–5 chalky-white eggs, incubated by both parents for 32–38 days. Chicks fledge at 8–9 weeks.

LIFESTYLE: The white stork feeds on wet grassland and marshes, covering the ground with long, stately strides as it searches for frogs, insects, and other prey to snap up with its long bill. It flies in a deceptively relaxed fashion, its head and neck outstretched and legs trailing, alternating a few wing flaps with long glides. It often soars high into the sky, circling on thermal upcurrents.

In many parts of its range it builds its huge stick nests on houses, church towers, and other buildings, where its presence is considered a sign of good luck. It performs a dramatic display on the nest, inflating its throat pouch and clapping or rattling its bill. Meanwhile it arches its head right over its back, then slowly returns it and reaches down towards its feet, rattling all the time. A mated pair of storks will often perform this display together, standing on the nest with their breasts touching.

The white stork is welcomed throughout its breeding range, and is often provided with artificial nesting platforms, but it has declined in many regions owing to the drainage of former wetlands to create farmland, and the increasing use of farm pesticides.

TAKING A BATH
The stork wades in the shallows when looking for prey such as frogs and fish, but only ventures into deeper water when it needs to bathe and preen its plumage.

ROSEATE SPOONBILL

Ajaia ajaja
Family: THRESKIORNITHIDAE
Order: CICONIIFORMES

DISTRIBUTION: Mainly on coastal lagoons and mangrove swamps, less frequently on lakes, marshes and other inland wetlands, from the southern United States and Caribbean region through Central and South America, south as far as north-western Peru and northern Argentina.

SIZE: Length 27–34in (69–87cm); weight 2.7–3.9lb (1.24–1.75kg).

APPEARANCE: Large brilliant pink wading bird with darker pink wings; bright red highlights on inner leading edge of wing and just above tail; long red legs, bare green skin on head (partly orange during courtship), and broad, flattened greenish-yellow bill (often spotted with black) that widens to a spatula-like shape at tip. In breeding season, head may turn buff, and there is a tuft of red feathers on breast. Immature birds have feathered heads, white plumage with variable pale pink on body and wings.

DIET: This spoonbill species eats mainly small fish; also other crustaceans (especially shrimps), water beetles, snails, mollusks, and other small invertebrates; small amounts of aquatic plant material, such as roots of sedges.

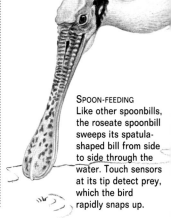

SPOON-FEEDING
Like other spoonbills, the roseate spoonbill sweeps its spatula-shaped bill from side to side through the water. Touch sensors at its tip detect prey, which the bird rapidly snaps up.

BREEDING: Season varies. Pair builds untidy nest of sticks, lined with soft vegetation. Nest in groups at tops of trees. 2–5 dull, dirty-white eggs, blotched and spotted brown, incubated by both parents for 21–24 days. Chicks fledge at about 6 weeks. Sexually mature by 3 years at earliest.

LIFESTYLE: The stunningly pink-hued roseate spoonbill is a highly gregarious bird, breeding, feeding and roosting in flocks, often in the company of other wading birds. The male cements his pair-bond by presenting sticks to his mate as she sits on the nest, accompanied by head-tossing, bowing, crossing and clattering their bills together, and strange, weak, grunting calls. The downy nestlings have stubby, soft bills that lack the characteristic spatulate tip. At just over a week after hatching, however, the tip starts to flatten, and by the time the youngster is 16 days old, its bill has the same shape as that of its parents. Early in the 20th century numbers were depleted by hunters, who slaughtered the birds to obtain their beautiful rich pink feathers for the lucrative plume trade; the wings, for instance, were made into ladies' fans. Protective legislation enabled the birds to make a comeback, but some populations suffer from drainage of wetlands, human disturbance and the effects of the pesticide DDT in their wintering areas.

GREATER FLAMINGO

Phoenicopterus ruber
Family: PHOENICOPTERIDAE
Order: CICONIIFORMES

DISTRIBUTION: Brackish or salty coastal lagoons and soda lakes in southern Europe, Africa, southwest Asia, Central America, West Indies, and Galápagos Islands.

SIZE: Length 49–57in (125–145cm); weight 4.6–9lb (2.1–4.1kg).

APPEARANCE: Extremely tall bird with very long neck and legs. Washed-out pink plumage with bright crimson wing-coverts, plus black primaries and secondaries. Grotesque down-turned bill, pink with black base.

DIET: Small crustaceans, mollusks, insects, aquatic worms, and microscopic organisms, plus seeds, plant fragments, and small fish.

BREEDING: In very large colonies in shallow water. Each pair builds a conical nest, usually of mud. 1 or 2 white, speckled eggs, incubated by female for 30–32 days. Chicks join crèche after 2–3 days, and become independent after 60 days.

LIFESTYLE: This extraordinary, yet graceful waterbird is restricted to shallow lakes and lagoons of salty or highly alkaline water, where it lives in spectacular flocks of hundreds or even thousands of birds. These flocks spend most of their time wading in the water, feeding by day or night. Each bird holds its bill upside down between its legs, sweeping it from side to side beneath the surface as it walks slowly forward. It uses its thick, muscular tongue to rapidly pump water in and out, and any edible particles are trapped on comb-like filters resembling those of plankton-feeding baleen whales. This feeding technique is best suited to catching small creatures up to about 1 inch (25mm) long.

Greater flamingoes fly well, often in lines or V-formations, their long necks and legs stretched out, and many temperate breeding populations migrate to warmer regions to spend the winter.

Within their large flocks smaller groups are formed. The groups display together, rhythmically "flagging" their heads from side to side and performing bowing and spread-wing poses. The pairs in each group may stay together for life, and all lay and incubate their eggs at the same time, so their young are all the same age. They feed their young on "crop-milk" – a protein-rich secretion from the parent bird's crop which ensures the chick gets a good start in life.

ROSE-TINTED DIET
The varied pink and crimson in the plumage of a greater flamingo is caused by pigments in the algae that it eats with its prey. The pigments resemble those in carrots.

MUTE SWAN

Cygnus olor
Family: ANATIDAE
Order: ANSERIFORMES

DISTRIBUTION: Fresh or brackish lakes and rivers from Britain, southern Scandinavia and the Baltic states to the Black Sea, Asia Minor, and central and eastern Asia. Introduced to parts of North America, Australia, New Zealand, and South Africa. Birds from northern and eastern areas winter farther south and west.

SIZE: Length 49–61in (125–155cm); weight 17–32lb (7.6–14.3kg).

APPEARANCE: Large waterbird with a long, slender neck and pointed tail. Pure white plumage; black legs and feet. Orange bill with black base and prominent black knob above base, larger in the male.

DIET: Aquatic plants and roots; grasses; also worms, shellfish, and other invertebrates.

BREEDING: Mute swans pair for life, and breed in spring. They build very large nest of sticks and reeds near water, with a hollow in the center that is thinly lined with down. 5–7 bluish-gray or bluish-green eggs, incubated by both parents for 34–38 days. The young are reared by both parents for about 4 months.

DULL JUVENILE
A juvenile mute swan is camouflaged with dingy gray-brown, and starts acquiring adult plumage during its first winter.

LIFESTYLE: The graceful, stately mute swan is a familiar ornamental bird in some parts of its range, where it frequently breeds on lakes in town parks. Wilder populations still live in many parts of Europe and Asia, where the birds form large flocks outside the breeding season. A mute swan often swims with its neck curved in an S-shape, unlike the more goose-like tundra swans. It feeds by reaching down to the bottom with its long neck while swimming on the surface, and often up-ends like a dabbling duck.

Its great weight makes take-off difficult, forcing a long run over the water with pattering feet. Once in the air the big, broad wings make a loud, rhythmic throbbing that is unique. Males become very aggressive in the breeding season, surging over the water to drive off intruders with their wings arched and necks curved back. They may even attack dogs and people who come too close to the nest. The downy young often climb onto their mother's back to shelter within her raised wings while she swims. Both parents stir up food for the young with their feet, or gather food from the bottom and pass it to them.

MALLARD

Anas platyrhynchos
Family: ANATIDAE
Order: ANSERIFORMES

DISTRIBUTION: Fresh and coastal waters throughout most of the Northern Hemisphere outside the tropics, except for the most northern parts of the tundra. Northern birds migrate south in winter. Introduced to Australasia.

SIZE: Length 20–25in (50–64cm); weight 1.6–3.5lb (0.7–1.6kg); male larger than female.

APPEARANCE: Male has greenish head, narrow white collar, gray back and underparts, dark purplish-brown breast, orange legs, and greenish-yellow bill. Female is mottled brown, with brown bill. Both have large blue wingpatch edged with white.

DIET: Wide range of land and water plants, seeds, and berries; also insects, crustaceans, mollusks, and other small aquatic animals.

BREEDING: Mainly in spring. The nest is a hollow in the ground, usually under a bush or hedge, lined with leaves and grass mixed with down and feathers. 7–12 greenish-gray to tawny-green or bluish eggs, incubated for 28–29 days. Young are led to the water soon after hatching, and fledge at 7–8 weeks.

LIFESTYLE: Although as wild as any other duck in many parts of its range, the adaptable, almost omnivorous mallard is a great opportunist, ready to breed on urban lakes and ponds, eat scraps and handouts, and even become tame enough to feed from the hand. Its flexibility has made it very successful, and the mallard is one of the most common and widespread of all waterbirds.

A mallard normally gathers food floating at or near the water surface by "dabbling" with its bill, either while wading in the shallows or swimming. The sides of its bill are lined with comb-like "lamellae" that act as filters, straining edible particles from the water. It also upends to take food from the bottom, but only if the water is less than about 18 inches (46cm) deep.

Mallard pair up briefly to mate. But once the females have eggs, the males form small flocks with other males, some of which are still unmated. The flocks harass and even rape females when they leave their eggs to find food, and these group attacks are sometimes fatal.

VARIABLE PLUMAGE
The mallard is the ancestor of most domestic ducks, and interbreeding causes many plumage variations. Most still have the blue wingpatch, but the white collar is often lost.

KING EIDER

> *Somateria spectabilis*
> Family: ANATIDAE
> Order: ANATIFORMES

DISTRIBUTION: Breeds across much of the high Arctic region, almost entirely north of the Arctic circle, from Alaska and northern Canada to Greenland, Iceland, and northern Russia; winters to the south, mainly at edge of pack ice.

SIZE: Length 18.5–25in (47–63cm); weight 3–4.5lb (1.4–2kg).

APPEARANCE: Large duck; male in breeding plumage has a bulbous, multicolored head, with a large orange knob at the base of his coral-red bill; a flat crown and nape, pale bluish with a purplish tinge; upper back and rump sides white; back black, with striking, triangular, black, sail-like feathers sticking up from shoulders; lower neck and breast salmon pink, rest of underparts black; wings look all black, but reveal a large white patch on each forewing in flight. Female is rusty brown, mottled with dark bars and crescents; juvenile like female but grayer.

DIET: Mainly mollusks, crustaceans, and sea urchins; also other small marine creatures and some plant matter; freshwater insects and larvae in the breeding season.

BREEDING: June-July. Nest on ground, often inland near a pool or other fresh water; usually among dense vegetation, a small hollow lined with down from female's breast and plant material; incubation 24–29 days; fledging 35–40 days.

LIFESTYLE: Among the most northerly of all birds, king eiders breed within a few hundred miles of the North Pole. They feed mainly in coastal waters, usually by diving to wrench or dig mollusks and other marine animals from the seabed with their strong bills,

PLUMAGE PURPOSES
The stunning male plumage evolved for impressing females. Females have a completely different, dull plumage for camouflage against predators, like Arctic foxes, when nesting.

which are also adapted for crushing the prey's shells.

It takes a male three years to attain his magnificent adult breeding plumage, passing through intermediate stages; the orange knob above the bill is clearly recognizable from their second summer onwards.

Although king eiders nest in isolated pairs, they are very gregarious outside the breeding season. They often flock with common eiders (*Somateria mollissima*).

Males abandon their mates after mating, leaving them to incubate the eggs and rear the ducklings on their own. The males travel to molt in huge numbers with other males at traditional sites. Like other wildfowl, they molt all their flight feathers together, so that they become flightless for a few weeks. During this vulnerable time, they acquire a duller, camouflaging "eclipse" plumage. Because the species lives in such remote and inhospitable regions, most rarely come into contact with humans, though some on migration are shot by hunters. A major oil spill from a tanker in the region of the vast molting or wintering flocks could kill huge numbers of birds.

CANADA GOOSE

Branta canadensis
Family: ANATIDAE
Order: ANSERIFORMES

DISTRIBUTION: Breeds on lakes and rivers in North America, from Alaska and Arctic Canada south to central United States. Introduced to northern Europe – mainly Britain and Scandinavia, but scattered elsewhere – and New Zealand.

SIZE: Length 22–43in (56–110cm); weight 8–12lb (3.7–5.4kg). Arctic races are the smallest; southern races the biggest.

APPEARANCE: Large, long-necked goose with swan-like proportions, long black bill, and black legs. Gray-brown body with white breast and rump; black neck and head with distinctive white "chinstrap." Dark flight feathers and tail.

DIET: Mainly plant material, such as roots, stems, leaves, fruits, and seeds, which it gathers on land. It may also take water plants by up-ending like a dabbling duck.

BREEDING: Nests in spring, in a colony on ground close to water, often on an island. Typically builds its nest at the base of a tree or bush, heaping up vegetation and lining the nesting hollow with down from the female's breast. 5–6 white or cream eggs, incubated by female for 28–30 days. Eggs hatch together, and goslings fledge at 40–48 days old. Young stay with parents throughout first winter.

LIFESTYLE: In their native North America many Canada geese are summer migrants to breeding grounds in the far north, and retreat south for the winter like other geese. In Europe they have abandoned migration, apart from short journeys to traditional molting sites, and live wild only in places where the climate is mild enough for year-round residence. They have also become extremely tolerant of people, breeding readily in places like urban parks, often in the centers of large cities. The Canada goose feeds mainly by grazing, and favors areas where there is plenty of open, level ground near lakes or slow-flowing rivers. It lives in flocks throughout most of the year, but the birds regularly confront each other when foraging with aggressive "head-pumping" displays, bobbing their heads up and down on their long, flexible, necks. Flocks often take to the air with loud, resonant, honking calls – the loudest of any goose.

SEMAPHORE SIGNAL
The bold, white "chinstrap" is vital to goose society, emphasizing the displays that allow dominant geese to pull rank on others.

WHOOPING CRANE

Grus americana
Family: GRUIDAE
Order: GRUIFORMES

DISTRIBUTION: Breeds on prairie wetlands, by shallow lakes and ponds, marshes, mudflats, and willow scrub. Only self-sustaining wild population breeds in Wood Buffalo National Park, on the border between Alberta and Northwest Territories, central Canada, and winters in and around Arkansas National Wildlife Refuge, Texas.

SIZE: Length 4.25–5.25ft (1.3–1.6m); weight 9.9–18.7lb (4.5–8.5kg).

APPEARANCE: Huge, white wading bird with long, sharply pointed bill and long legs; crown red; forehead, area between bill and eye, and mustache stripe black. Latter with red tip; bare red skin on face around horn-colored bill. Reveals black primary wing feathers in flight. Immature has brown feathers in wings and pale red-brown head.

DIET: Includes insects, small fish, frogs, small birds and rodents, berries in summer; clams, crabs and other animals in winter.

BREEDING: In spring. Both sexes build the large nest of wetland plants on the ground, often surrounded by water; it is up to 5 feet (1.5m) across and 1.5 feet (45cm) above water. Usually 2 buff to olive-buff eggs, marked with brown, reddish, and pale purplish spots, incubated by both sexes for 28–31 days. Young leave nest soon after hatching; fledge at 80–90 days.

LIFESTYLE: The tallest North American bird, the whooping crane is a majestic sight, both on the ground, where it walks with slow, measured strides, and in the air, flying with strong, rhythmic beats of great wings that span 7 feet (2.2m) or more. Groups perform wild dances and have far-carrying, trumpeting calls. The whooping crane once bred across the northern plains and prairies of North America. In the late 19th and early 20th centuries, as settlers hunted the birds and converted the wilderness for agriculture, numbers declined rapidly. By the late 1930s, the species was on the brink of extinction. Thanks to a sustained conservation effort, it is on the road to recovery, with almost 200 individuals in the wild.

PROBING FOR PREY
The whooping crane feeds mainly by probing gently with its long spike of a bill in the bottom mud of shallow wetlands, snapping up a variety of small animals, from crabs to fish.

BLACK COOT

Fulica atra
Family: RALLIDAE
Order: GRUIFORMES

DISTRIBUTION: Freshwater ponds, lakes, and marshes from the British Isles and southern Scandinavia south to northwest Africa and east to Asia and Australia.

SIZE: Length 17in (43cm); weight 1.2–2.5lb (0.56–1.15kg).

APPEARANCE: Black with white bill and forehead shield; narrow white edges to primaries visible in flight; legs greenish; red eyes.

DIET: Waterweeds, grasses, seeds; insects, worms, water snails.

BREEDING: In spring both birds build a floating nest of stems and leaves in vegetation by lake or marsh. 5–15 grayish-buff eggs, covered in dark brown and black speckles and spots. Eggs incubated by both parents for 21–24 days. Chicks brooded by female, fed by both parents for first month.

LIFESTYLE: Widespread waterbird, the black coot is highly social in

winter but territorial and quarrelsome in summer during the breeding season. Winter flocks of a thousand or more may gather on inland lakes, often concentrated on remaining patches of open water by the freezing of smaller lakes and ponds. They dive for food, flattening their feathers to expel the air before taking off and plunging down, propelled by the broad lobes on their big, powerful feet. They bounce back up like corks, the water instantly streaming off their plumage. As food becomes harder to find in winter they may get quite tame, especially in areas where they are used to people, and they often gather to take food from the hand like domestic ducks.

During the breeding season black coots change their character. Both sexes become intensely territorial, defending their boundaries with aggressive displays that often lead

to fights. Rivals swim at each other with their heads down, tails raised, and wings arched, or even run across the water flapping their wings. Often an intruder will turn tail and run, but many stand their ground and fight, leaping from the water and slashing with their sharp claws. Territorial coots will even attack other species, with such ferocity that they have been known to drive away full-grown swans. Adaptable and opportunistic, black coots often nest on lakes in urban parks, and they are quick to

FRONTAL ATTACK
A black coot uses its bold white forehead shield as a territorial signal, displaying it at rivals and intruders before spreading its wings and leaping into the attack with its sharp claws.

colonize new reservoirs, or flooded gravel or sand pits. Severe, icy winters can hit black coots hard, but their populations usually recover well within a few years.

LIMPKIN

Aramus guarauna
Family: ARAMIDAE
Order: GRUIFORMES

DISTRIBUTION: Swamps, marshes, and shores of lakes and slow-moving rivers, from Florida and the Caribbean islands south to northern Argentina, excluding areas west of the Andes.

SIZE: Length 22–28in (56–71cm); weight 2.2–3lb (1–1.37kg).

APPEARANCE: Long-legged wading bird, with short, rounded wings, short broad tail, and long, flattened, slightly down-curved bill. Plumage dark brown, variably streaked with white; legs blackish-green; bill dark yellowish, with a darker, grayish tip; eyes hazel brown.

DIET: Usually almost entirely apple snails; sometimes other water snails, mussels, crayfish, small lizards, and other small animals.

BREEDING: Varies with region. Pair builds flimsy nest of sticks in a bush or tree, on a heap of aquatic vegetation or on ground. 4–8 pale creamy-buff or olive-buff eggs, spotted and blotched with various shades of brown and lilac; incubated by both parents. May breed 2 or 3 times a year.

LIFESTYLE: The only member of its family, the limpkin looks like an ibis or an overgrown, long-legged member of the rail family; it also shares some features with cranes. Although it sometimes takes other prey, the limpkin is a highly specialized feeder. Its staple food over most of its range is a particular type of large freshwater snail, the apple snail. In a few places, such as the Caribbean, it may eat small land animals where it occurs away from water, and elsewhere, during periods of drought or flooding, it can switch to feeding on other prey, including land snails, earthworms, and slugs. The limpkin's long legs enable it to wade deeply in the water. Its long, slim toes and long, sharp claws enable it to perch and clamber about in trees, and walk on floating mats of vegetation. It finds the snails by probing deeply into the mud with its long bill or picking them from vegetation, and it carries each catch to the shore. Here, it inserts its bill into the mollusk's shell and neatly cuts the muscle before removing and devouring the animal's soft body.

WEIRD CHORUS
The cacophony made by male limpkins defending their territories with loud, wailing, shrieking, and rattling calls is one of the strangest sounds in nature. It is often heard through the night.

PALEARCTIC OYSTERCATCHER

Haematopus ostralegus
Family: HAEMATOPODIDAE
Order: CHARADRIIFORMES

DISTRIBUTION: Breeds along coasts and on shingle and sand bars along inland rivers, from Europe and Scandinavia east to the Urals and Asia Minor, parts of central Asia, the Kamchatka Peninsula, and around the coasts of the Yellow Sea. Winters farther south to northern Africa, Arabia, India, and southeast China.

SIZE: Length 17in (43cm); weight 15–24oz (430–675g).

APPEARANCE: Large shore bird with very striking black-and-white plumage, long orange bill, and pink legs. Black head, neck, and back, with white wingbar visible in flight; white belly and underwing. Throat black in summer, white in winter. Eyes red, with distinct orange rim.

DIET: Mollusks such as mussels and cockles; marine worms, insects, and other invertebrates.

BREEDING: In spring. Makes scrape on shingle, sand, among rocks, or in vegetation, sometimes lining the scrape with dead plant material or small stones. 2–4 pale buff eggs, spotted and blotched with black, incubated by both parents for 24–27 days. Chicks leave nest at 1–2 days, and are fed and guarded by both parents. They fledge at about 5 weeks.

LIFESTYLE: Noisy and gregarious. the palearctic oystercatcher is a conspicuous part of the seashore wildlife on coasts throughout much of Europe and Asia. It attracts attention by calling noisily in flight with a shrill, piping "kleep kleep," and flocks of flying birds can be dazzling to watch as their white wingbars flash in the sun.

They usually roost in large, dense flocks, and feed in loose groups on rocky, sandy, or muddy shores. Some birds specialize in gathering soft-bodied prey such as marine worms, by probing in soft beach sediments, and these have pointed

WINTER FLOCKS
Huge flocks of migrant
oystercatchers gather on
mild coasts in winter, when
the bird develops a thin
white collar on its normally
black neck.

bills. Others feed by
hammering into mussels
and other mollusks, and
these have chisel-tipped bills.
Since the outer sheath of the bill
grows continuously, like our
fingernails, it can adapt to suit the
bird's preferred feeding technique.
Shellfish-feeders also adopt one of
two methods of opening bivalve
mollusks such as cockles and
mussels. They either smash the
shells by hammering them with their
bills, or stab between the shells to
cut the muscle that holds them
closed. Each bird learns one of
these techniques from its parents,
and uses it for the rest of its life.
The adults dispute breeding territory
with a noisy "piping display," in
which either the male or both birds
threaten intruders by circling with
their heads lowered and bills
pointing down and slightly open – all
the while giving bursts of piercing
piping calls. Males also perform in
the air, giving wailing cries while
flying with slow, stiff wingbeats.

LAPWING

Vanellus vanellus
Family: CHARADRIIDAE
Order: CHARADRIIFORMES

DISTRIBUTION: Breeds across much of northern Europe and Asia, in temperate zone east to China. Northern birds winter in western and southern Europe, the Middle East, India, and southern China.

SIZE: Length 11–12in (28–31cm); weight 5.3–10.6oz (150–300g).

APPEARANCE: Large plover, with distinctive wispy crest and broad, rounded wings. Bronze-green upper parts, black chest, white belly;

reddish-buff under tail. Buff, black, and white face, with less buff in summer. Breeding male has black throat, and iridescent blue sheen on shoulders. Short black bill; dark pink legs.

DIET: Mainly insects, spiders, earthworms, and mollusks; also some small fish and frogs.

BREEDING: In spring, male makes several scrapes on open ground, lining them with grass on wet sites. The female chooses one, and lays 3–5 buff to pale brown eggs, heavily blotched with dark brown to black. Incubation 21–28 days, mainly by female. Chicks find own food; fledge at 35–40 days.

LIFESTYLE: Outside the breeding season northern lapwings gather in

IRIDESCENT SHEEN
Although it looks black and white from a distance, a northern lapwing in breeding plumage glows with iridescent green, bronze, and blue at close range. Its long, wispy crest is unique in Europe.

large, loose flocks on estuaries, coastal marshes, and farmland. They often feed on plowed fields, running forward and tilting over to seize insect grubs and earthworms. They spend a lot of time standing still, often in flocks of hundreds or even thousands. In flight they are distinctive; their slow, rhythmic, rather floppy wingbeats creating a twinkly effect as they flash black and white. They also have a characteristic "peewit" call.

In spring the males perform wonderful aerial displays in which they dive, swerve, and tumble through the sky, calling with loud "whee-er-ee-vip-a-vip," their flight feathers humming. When their chicks hatch and start feeding in the open, the adults defend them by diving on predators with shrill cries, or distracting them with broken-wing displays; meanwhile the well-camouflaged chicks crouch down out of sight.

Lapwings belong to the plover family of small to medium wading birds. Several species have crests. While still common, northern lapwings have been badly affected by modern farming methods and land drainage schemes, which have destroyed many of their former breeding sites on wet grassland.

COMMON SNIPE

Gallinago gallinago
Family: SCOLOPACIDAE
Order: CHARADRIIFORMES

DISTRIBUTION: Breeds in marshes and damp open country throughout northern North America, Europe, and Asia. Winters near fresh water farther south to northernmost South America, north and central Africa, the Middle East, and southeast Asia.

SIZE: Length 10–10.5in (25–27cm); weight 4–4.5oz (113–128g).

APPEARANCE: Quite small wading bird with very long, straight bill and strongly striped plumage. Rich brown above with cream stripes; black crown with cream central stripe; sides of head brown with cream stripes above and below eye; reddish tail patch with white tip; pale, mottled breast; white belly. Pale green legs, blackish bill, and dark eyes.

DIET: Mainly earthworms, insects, mollusks, crustaceans; some seeds.

BREEDING: In spring, female makes shallow scrape lined with grass.

3–4 pale green, olive, or buff eggs, marked with shades of brown, olive, and purplish-gray, incubated by female alone for 18–20 days. Young leave nest soon after hatching and are reared by both parents. Fledge at 19–20 days.

LIFESTYLE: Superbly camouflaged by its cryptic plumage, the snipe can be hard to see as it hunts for worms, grubs, and other prey among the vegetation of marshes and wet grassland. It feeds by rapidly probing the soft mud with its long bill, often making many deep probes in a circle as it stands in one place. It feels for prey with its sensitive bill tip, and is able to catch and swallow small animals without withdrawing its bill. Bigger victims such as earthworms are hauled out and often immobilized by repeated hammering before being swallowed whole.

At any sign of danger it lies low and usually stays undetected, but if

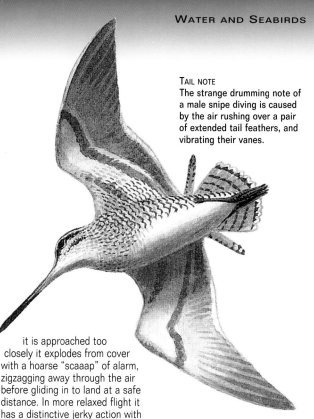

TAIL NOTE
The strange drumming note of a male snipe diving is caused by the air rushing over a pair of extended tail feathers, and vibrating their vanes.

it is approached too closely it explodes from cover with a hoarse "scaaap" of alarm, zigzagging away through the air before gliding in to land at a safe distance. In more relaxed flight it has a distinctive jerky action with fast, flickering beats of its sharp-pointed wings.

Snipe of both sexes often display near their nest sites by perching on posts or large clods of earth and giving a loud, rhythmic "chip-a chip-a" song. On warm evenings in spring and summer the males also perform dramatic aerial displays over their territory – rising, circling, and then diving with a weird, tremulous drumming sound produced by their vibrating tail feathers.

DUNLIN

Calidris alpina
Family: SCOLOPACIDAE
Order: CHARADRIIFORMES

DISTRIBUTION: Breeds throughout the far north and in some northern temperate regions, from Arctic tundra to damp moorland and grassy saltmarsh. Winters on estuaries and wetland from southern Canada, Britain, and Japan south to Mexico, West Africa, India and south China.

SIZE: Length 6–8.5in (16–22cm); weight 1.4–1.8oz (40–50g).

APPEARANCE: A small, round-shouldered shorebird with a slim, longish, slightly downcurved bill. In summer has rich chestnut and black on crown and back; pale, dark-streaked breast; black belly. In winter gray-brown above; gray-streaked breast; white belly. Narrow white wingbar and white underwing in all plumages.

DIET: Mollusks, crustaceans, worms, and insects.

BREEDING: In spring. Nest is a shallow cup of grasses or leaves concealed in a grass tussock; 3–4 pale green eggs, spotted with dark brown; incubation 21–22 days, by both sexes; chicks active soon after hatching, and find own food; fledge in 19–21 days.

LIFESTYLE: The dunlin is a very abundant shorebird throughout the Northern Hemisphere. In winter it often gathers on the coasts of North America, Europe, and Asia in vast flocks of tens of thousands, especially on muddy estuaries. The birds return to the same wintering ground each year after breeding in the far north. The various winter populations do not mix, and there are several races; American and east Siberian birds are much bigger than those that winter in Europe.

Dunlins are energetic feeders, running about and using their bills to probe the tidal mud with a rapid repeat action. The winter flocks are spectacular in flight, twisting and turning in tight, coordinated maneuvers, their massed wings flashing gray and white in the low winter sun.

In spring most dunlins migrate north to breed on the tundra, although some breed on moorlands and marshes in Britain and around the Baltic. They nest in loose colonies, and each male performs a switchback display flight over the nesting site to claim his territory. The nestings develop rapidly in the brief summer to beat the onset of winter.

SUMMER DRESS
The rich chestnut plumage of a breeding dunlin is replaced in winter by a more restrained gray above and white below – although the white often gleams brightly in the sun.

STONE CURLEW

> *Burhinus oedicnemus*
> Family: BURHINIDAE
> Order: CHARADRIIFORMES

DISTRIBUTION: A relative of wading birds, this species breeds in open country with short vegetation, bare sand or shingle, or in scrub from western Europe to Central Asia, India, Indochina, and Africa.

SIZE: Length 16–17in (40–44cm); weight 10.2–18.9oz (290–535g).

APPEARANCE: Heavy-bodied, long-legged bird with quite short, strong bill and big, staring, yellow eyes. Light brown above, flecked and streaked with darker brown; white wingbar bordered with black, visible when standing; two white wingbars and dark leading edge in flight; belly and flanks white. Yellow legs; bill short and straight, with black tip and yellow base.

DIET: Earthworms, insects, and mollusks; sometimes mice, young birds, and lizards.

BREEDING: In spring. Nest is a shallow scrape on the ground, unlined or thinly lined with plant fragments, small stones, or rabbit dung. 2–3 whitish to pale brown eggs, mottled and streaked with brown and gray, incubated by both parents for 25–27 days. Chicks fledge in 36–42 days

LIFESTYLE: The strange-looking stone curlew is a secretive, mainly nocturnal bird of sandy heaths, stony grasslands, and arable fields. It spends most of the day doing very little, but becomes active at night when its large eyes enable it to target prey such as beetles, grubs, earthworms, and even mice. It searches the ground rapidly and can run fast in pursuit of prey, its outstretched head lowered ready to seize its victims in its strong bill. It often takes to the air on long, pointed wings at dusk, flying high with a wailing "kierr-lee" call rather like that of the curlew – which accounts for its name.

Stone curlews are sociable birds that form flocks in the fall and winter. They may even feed in groups during the breeding season, and neighboring pairs regularly gather for group displays when they leap, call loudly, run about, and charge at each other. These performances may last for over half an hour before the pairs disperse to return to their nests.

LOCAL DECLINES
Although it is still common in some areas, the stone curlew has declined in regions where intensive farming has destroyed its wild grassland habitat.

Pied Avocet

Recurvirostra avosetta
Family: RECURVIROSTRIDAE
Order: CHARADRIIFORMES

DISTRIBUTION: Breeds on a variety of freshwater or brackish wetlands, both coastal and inland, across Eurasia from southeast England to the Far East. Most populations winter farther south, in Africa and the Middle East.

SIZE: Length 16.5–18in (42–45cm); weight 8–15.4oz (228–435g).

APPEARANCE: Long-legged wader with slender upcurved bill and webbed feet. Plumage mainly white, with black on crown and nape extending to bill and just below eye, and black bands on wings and wingtips. Bluish-gray legs; black bill; brown eyes.

DIET: Crustaceans, mollusks, worms, and insects.

BREEDING: In spring, makes a shallow scrape on bare ground or in short vegetation near water's edge; nest unlined or thinly lined with dead plant material. 3–5 pale brownish-buff eggs, with small

BUFF AND BROWN
Adult pied avocets have pure white and jet-black plumage, but immature birds like this one are smudged with buff on their backs and the dark areas of their plumage are a dull dark brown. Both have the characteristic upcurved bill.

spots and blotches of black or gray, incubated by both parents for 22–24 days. Young leave nest soon after hatching, and fledge at 35–42 days.

LIFESTYLE: The slim, elegant pied avocet uses its pointed, upcurved bill to sift through shallow water and thin mud for small animals such as shrimps, sweeping it from side to side with a brisk flicking action. It leans forward to feed, so the end of the slightly open bill is horizontal with the water surface, maximizing its chances of catching prey. It also swims in deeper water, upending like a duck to reach prey beneath the surface. In winter it often gathers in large groups of several hundred birds to feed on favored estuaries. Its plumage can look dazzling in bright sunlight, especially in flight when its black wingtips create a flickering effect against the white. It calls with a loud, liquid, fluty "kleep."

Always sociable, the pied avocet nests in dense colonies of up to 200 pairs, often on muddy islets. Each pair defends its nest site, but the whole colony join together to drive away intruders. Its breeding range in western Europe has increased in recent decades, mainly because of protection on bird reserves.

LONG-TAILED JAEGER

Stercorarius longicaudus
Family: STERCORARIIDAE
Order: CHARADRIIFORMES

DISTRIBUTION: Breeds on tundra throughout the high Arctic. Winters in the southern Pacific and southern Atlantic Oceans.

SIZE: Length 19.5–23in (50–58cm); weight 8.3–12.6oz (236–358 g).

APPEARANCE: A small, elegant, slightly-built seabird with long narrow wings. Breeding adult has very long central tail streamers, which extend up to 7 inches (18 cm) beyond rest of tail. Dark brown above, with blackish-brown crown, wing tips and tail, and pale yellow sides of neck; white below, with dark underwing; very occasionally much darker; slatey-gray to black legs; black bill; dark brown eyes.

DIET: Mainly fish and marine invertebrates outside breeding season; feeds on lemmings and insects on tundra during breeding season. May steal prey from other birds – a common trait among its larger skua relatives.

BREEDING: Gather in loose colonies in Arctic summer and nest in a shallow scrape, unlined or thinly lined with plant material, in peat or moss. Two eggs, olive-green to olive-brown or buff; spotted, blotched, or scrawled with brown or pale gray, especially around larger end; incubated by both parents for about 23 days. Young leave nest after 2 days.

LIFESTYLE: The jaegers are small skuas, close relatives of the gulls,

WHIPPING UP INTEREST
The very long tail streamers of a breeding adult add drama to its aerial displays, whipping about in the air as the bird soars and glides over its nesting and feeding territory on the tundra.

that often force other bird species to disgorge their food in flight. The long-tailed jaeger is the smallest and slimmest, resembling a tern as it soars gracefully over the water or hovers over the tundra watching for prey. It is also less piratical than other jaegers and skuas, although it occasionally steals prey from neighboring terns. In the short Arctic summer it hunts lemmings for itself and its young by hovering above them and then swooping in for the kill, pursuing them on the ground and killing them with its bill. When lemmings are numerous,

they breed successfully, but in years when lemmings are scarce the jaegers may not breed at all. The "boom and bust" lemming cycle is a normal part of life on the Arctic tundra, and the jaegers prepare for it by incubating the first egg as soon as it is laid, rather than waiting for the second. It hatches first, and the elder chick may then kill the younger one if there is not enough food, ensuring that at least one chick survives.

ARCTIC TERN

Sterna paradisaea
Family: STERNIDAE
Order: CHARADRIIFORMES

DISTRIBUTION: Breeds on marshy tundra and saltmarshes throughout the Arctic and sub-Arctic, and on rocky beaches and moorland in parts of northern Europe. Spends the northern winter in the far south, in the Southern Ocean around the Antarctic pack ice.

SIZE: Length 13–15in (33–38cm); weight 3–4.5oz (86–127g).

APPEARANCE: Round-headed, long-winged tern with long, whippy tail streamers. Medium gray above, with paler underparts; crown and nape black; underwing has narrow black band on trailing edge. Legs and bill deep red; bill black outside breeding season.

DIET: Small fish, crustaceans, and insects.

BREEDING: in northern summer. Forms large breeding colonies, sometimes with other seabirds. Nest a shallow scrape made by female, on ground or in moss, unlined or thinly lined with plant material, small pebbles, or shells. 1–3 bluish-white, greenish, buff, cream, or deep brown eggs, speckled, blotched, and scribbled with dark brown, black, or olive. Incubated by both parents for 20–22 days. Young leave nest soon after hatching, and are cared for by both parents until they fledge at 21–26 days.

LIFESTYLE: Superficially similar to their relatives the gulls, terns are smaller and more delicate, with slender bodies, narrow wings, forked tails, and slim, pointed bills. The Arctic tern is one of the "sea terns," which hunt by hovering above the waves and plunging down to catch small fish. Its hunting style is strangely hesitant; it often swoops down for prey in a series of steps, hovering between each as if to check that it is still on target. Finally it dives right in to seize its prey in its bill.

True to its name, the Arctic tern breeds mainly in the Arctic region, but also on boulder-strewn shores and bleak moorland in Ireland, Scotland, the Faeroes, and around the North Sea and Baltic. It may breed in large colonies, vigorously defending its nests against predators and other intruders by diving at them and striking them with its sharp bill, calling all the while with a rasping "kee-yah."

Outside the breeding season the Arctic tern feeds entirely at sea, resting on ice-floes and other floating objects. In the fall it makes the longest migration known for any bird, flying south for some 10,000 miles (16,000km) to spend the northern winter months at the edge of the Antarctic pack-ice. Since it is summer in the Antarctic, with almost 24-hour daylight, and the tern returns north only when the same is true in the Arctic, it experiences more hours of daylight each year than any other animal.

FISH FAMINE
Arctic terns eat small fish such as sandeels. A serious decline in numbers around Britain in the 1980s has been blamed on a crash in sandeel stocks, probably caused by overfishing.

HERRING GULL

Larus argentatus
Family: LARIDAE
Order: CHARADRIIFORMES

DISTRIBUTION: Breeds on cliff ledges, shingle, dunes, islands, and buildings throughout much of the northern hemisphere, from Europe and Scandinavia through Siberia to Alaska, Canada, and the United States. Winters along coasts, and around inland lakes. Some birds move south toward the subtropics in winter.

SIZE: Length 22–26in (56–66cm); weight 26.5–44oz (750–1,250g).

APPEARANCE: Large, strongly-built gull with big head and powerful bill. Very variable in size and color, but adult bird always has white head, streaked with brown in winter; wings and back dark to silvery-gray, with white-spotted, black wingtips. White underparts. Pink legs and feet; yellow bill with red spot near tip. Juvenile mottled gray-brown, with dark bill.

DIET: Mainly fish, crustaceans, and mollusks; also other birds, eggs, and young. Scavenges on refuse and carrion, and steals food from other seabirds.

BREEDING: In spring and summer. Nests in colonies. Each pair builds large nest of seaweed, grass, and debris in a scrape or hollow. 2–3 pale olive, buff, green, or brown eggs; blotched, speckled, and spotted with black, blackish-brown, or dark olive. Incubated by both parents, especially female, for 25–33 days. Young are cared for by both parents, and fledge at about 6 weeks.

LIFESTYLE: One of the biggest, toughest, and noisiest of the gulls, the herring gull is also one of the most successful. Essentially a predator and scavenger, it has learned to exploit a wide variety of foods, from fish caught at sea to edible refuse taken from urban garbage dumps. This flexibility has allowed it to colonize a wide variety of habitats, especially outside the breeding season when many move inland to feed on fields or in towns. It often occurs in large winter roosts on reservoirs and lakes.

During the breeding season it is more restricted to coasts, favoring rocky shores with cliffs and stacks that offer plenty of good nesting sites. But it still gathers food in coastal towns, or from around fishing ports and processing plants. It may even breed on urban sites. In some cities it is regarded as a pest because its droppings foul buildings, but despite some local attempts at control it has enjoyed a widespread increase in numbers throughout the last century.

SOUND OF THE SEA
The "kyeow-yow-yow" of the herring gull is one of the most evocative of all coastal sounds in the northern hemisphere.

BLACK SKIMMER

Rynchops niger
Family: RYNCHOPIDAE
Order: CHARADRIIFORMES

DISTRIBUTION: Sheltered inshore waters along coasts, estuaries, and lagoons; also large rivers and lakes; breeds in the United States, along the Pacific coast of southern California, and on the Atlantic coast from Massachusetts south to Florida, also in South America from Colombia to northern Argentina; winters to south of breeding range, including in Central America.

SIZE: Length 16–18in (41–46cm); weight 8–10oz (235–295g); male larger than female.

APPEARANCE: Long-winged, with short legs and heavy head; the big bill is flattened sideways, with the lower mandible longer than the upper one. Plumage black on crown, back and upperwings, with white face and underparts; legs red; bill red with black tip. In winter, adults have a white collar; juveniles mottled dull brown above.

DIET: Mainly small fish; also shrimps and other crustaceans.

BREEDING: In spring and summer. Forms compact breeding colonies, often near other seabirds. Nest an unlined scrape in sand or shell debris above high-tide mark. 3–5 whitish or buff eggs, heavily spotted, blotched and scribbled with dark brown, purple and gray, incubated by both parents, especially female, for 21–23 days. Young fledge in 23–25 days; cared for by both parents.

LIFESTYLE: This odd-looking bird is named for its remarkable habit of skimming the water when feeding. Its favourite prey is small fish, such as anchovies, minnows, killifishes, and silversides.

The black skimmer feeds mainly at dusk and dawn, and on moonlit nights. Its eyes have big pupils, so it can see in dim light. To prevent it being dazzled by brilliant sunlight during the day, the pupils do not contract to a circle as in other birds, but narrow to vertical slits,

so less light reaches the retina. Feeding after dark helps the skimmer avoid competing with other fish-eating birds that hunt during the day. The young hatch with mandibles of equal length, and can pick up food dropped on ground in front of them, which their parents are unable to do. By the time the young skimmer takes its first flight, at almost a month old, the lower mandible is noticeably longer, and it continues to grow until it reaches adult proportions after a further three months.

UNIQUE FEEDER
Flying only inches above the water, the skimmer shears the surface with the long lower mandible of its bladelike bill. As soon as this touches prey, the bird snaps its bill shut to trap it.

ATLANTIC PUFFIN

Fratercula arctica
Family: ALCIDAE
Order: CHARADRIIFORMES

DISTRIBUTION: Breeds on clifftops around coasts and islands of North Atlantic, from northeast North America and Greenland to Svalbard and Novaya Zemlya. Winters farther south.

SIZE: Length 11–12in (28–30cm); weight 13.4oz (381g).

APPEARANCE: Stocky seabird with a large head and short wings. Short legs set well back, giving an upright stance on land. Breeding plumage black on head, back, wings, and tail, with large white cheek patches and white underparts. Very large bill, flattened sideways, striped with red, yellow, and gray or blue. Yellow eye with red eye-ring and horny blue ornaments; orange-red legs. Face dusky in winter, and bill smaller and duller.

DIET: Small fish such as sandeels and capelin, mollusks, crustaceans, and other marine invertebrates, which it catches by swimming underwater using its wings.

BREEDING: Atlantic puffins breed in summer in large clifftop colonies. They excavate burrows or use old rabbit or shearwater burrows, natural hollows or rock crevices. The nest is a shallow scrape deep inside the tunnel or crevice, scattered with plant material. 1 white egg (rarely 2), often with faint brown or purplish blotches, incubated by both parents, but mainly by female, for 40–43 days. Chick cared for by both parents, but deserted in 40 days.

LIFESTYLE: Although it may look like a toy, the Atlantic puffin is a superbly adapted hunter, capable of "flying" underwater in pursuit of small fish and catching a dozen or more at a time in its deep, sharp-edged bill. Its wings are quite small to make them usable underwater, and this reduces their efficiency in the air, forcing the puffin to fly with fast, whirring wingbeats that only add to its toylike character.

In spring its bill becomes encased in gaudily striped horny plates, and it grows small horny ornaments above and below its eyes. Each year these adornments become bigger and brighter. They play a vital part in courtship, but they are discarded in winter when the puffins leave their clifftop colonies and live out on the open ocean.

Atlantic puffin colonies are often targeted by predators like great skuas and great black-backed gulls, which steal their fish and prey on their young. They can also suffer from food shortages, caused by climatic changes as well as the activities of north Atlantic fishing fleets, and some colonies have suffered serious declines.

FISH TRAP
Normally a puffin swallows its catch underwater but in the breeding season it carries 10–30 fish back to the nest, secured by spines lining its upper bill.

ANDEAN CONDOR

Vultur gryphus
Family: CATHARTIDAE
Order: FALCONIFORMES

DISTRIBUTION: The high Andes mountains of South America, from western Venezuela south to Tierra del Fuego.

SIZE: Length 43in (110cm); weight 21–30lb (9.5–13.5kg).

APPEARANCE: Very large vulture; with long square-tipped wings and broad tail. Glossy black with silvery-gray wing coverts and white ruff around neck, not quite meeting in front. Head and neck bare, with reddish skin; male has fleshy dark red or black comb. White bill, brown eyes, and gray legs.

DIET: Carrion, refuse, and some weak or sick animals; also birds' eggs on the seabird colonies of coastal Peru.

BREEDING: Breeds every other year, in spring, in mountain cave or cleft of rock. 1 (rarely 2) white eggs, incubated by both parents for 54–58 days. Chick reared by both parents. Fledges at 16 months.

LIFESTYLE: The largest of all birds of prey, and one of the biggest of all flying birds, the majestic Andean condor has become the unofficial emblem of the rugged Andes mountains. Wings outstretched, it soars for hours around the cliffs and crags, using its excellent eyesight to detect carrion from a great height. Like other vultures it is always alert to the activity of other birds, and quick to join other scavengers as they spiral down to feed on dead animals such as llamas or stray domestic sheep and cattle. It has a keen eye for disease or injury, and sometimes lands near sick animals and waits for them to die. It may have to wait even longer, because although its powerful hooked bill is an effective butcher's tool, it cannot deal with the thickest hide until it starts to decompose. Sometimes groups of condors feed together from large carcasses, gorging themselves to the point where they cannot take

off from flat ground. Food is often scarce in the mountains, and the condors make the most of every meal.

Although most of its diet consists of carrion, the Andean condor occasionally kills and eats live prey. These are usually weakened animals that would die anyway, but this habit has made it unpopular with farmers and ranchers, and many are shot. They also react badly to disturbance at their nesting cliffs, and since they breed slowly – rearing just one chick every other year – breeding failures are a serious problem. So although it is not under serious threat, it is in decline.

CLEAN SHAVEN
The bare skin on the condor's head and neck enable it to thrust its heavy hooked bill deep within a carcass without getting its plumage matted with blood – a valuable adaptation for a scavenger.

LAMMERGEIER

Gypaetus barbatus
Family: ACCIPITRIDAE
Order: ACCIPITRIFORMES

DISTRIBUTION: Areas of high mountains with numerous cliffs and gorges, locally at desert wadis (dry riverbeds) with high, rocky walls, and high steppes; from southern Europe and Africa to Middle East, central Asia, the Himalayan region, Tibet, Mongolia and north China.

SIZE: Length 37–49in (94–125cm); weight 11–15lb (5–6.7kg).

APPEARANCE: A huge vulture with a "beard" of bristly black feathers, long, narrow, pointed wings and long, diamond-shaped tail. Back, wings and tail blackish-gray; crown and face dirty white, with black band through eye; underparts usually tawny (color acquired by bathing in iron-rich spring water or dust), with black streaks and spots on chest in Eurasian and northwest African race; legs feathered, feet dark gray; powerful bill; eyes cream to yellow with red outer ring. Juvenile all-dark, with blackish head and upperparts, spotted with white, and grey-brown underparts.

DIET: Mostly flesh and bones from animal carcasses; scavenges waste human food at village garbage dumps, even in towns in Ethiopia.

BREEDING: Season varies. Nest, high on a mountain ledge or cave in a sheer cliff, a massive pile of branches, lined with wool, animal dung, dried skin, and sometimes rubbish. 1–2 whitish eggs, blotched with brown or purple, incubated by female for 53–60 days. Usually only one chick is reared, by both parents; fledges at 100–130 days.

LIFESTYLE: The lammergeier (or bearded vulture) is among the world's biggest, most impressive birds of prey. A superbly skilled flier, it spends much of the day in the air. Its unique diet includes much bone as well as carrion. It waits until other vultures have finished feeding at a carcass, then picks at any remaining meat and removes the bones. It swallows

small ones whole, but flies up with larger bones and drops them up to 20 times or more onto rocks until they shatter, then swoops down to eat the rich marrow within and devour the bone fragments. It also preys on tortoises and small mammals, dropping them on rocks to break their shells or kill them.

Sadly, this magnificent creature has suffered massive declines due to a variety of human impacts. Chief among them are poisoning when the birds eat baits set out by farmers to kill wolves and other predators; shooting; habitat degradation, disturbance at nest sites, lack of suitable food; and collisions with power cables.

SCARCE SCAVENGER
This unusual vulture is very sparsely distributed, since each pair needs a vast home range for survival – typically as much as 240 square miles (625sq km) in area.

SECRETARY BIRD

Sagittarius serpentarius
Family: SAGITTARIIDAE
Order: FALCONIFORMES

DISTRIBUTION: Wide variety of grasslands, savannas, and cultivated land in tropical Africa south of the Sahara.

SIZE: Length 49–59in (125–150cm); weight 7.5–8.4lb (3.4–3.8kg).

APPEARANCE: A tall, slender, very long-legged raptor with long wings, a long tail with long central feathers, and small feet. It owes its odd name to the quills of its crest of long, loose black feathers, which reminded early naturalists of the quill pens that 19th-century secretaries kept behind their ears for convenience. Plumage bluish-gray with grayish-white underparts; tail black, white, and gray. Bright pink bare skin on face. Brown eyes, dark gray bill, and pink legs.

DIET: Large insects, lizards, small mammals, snakes, young birds, and birds' eggs.

BREEDING: Nests in May or June, building a platform of sticks up to 8ft (2.4m) across, up to 40ft (12m) above ground in tree or on cliff. 2–3 whitish, pinkish or buff eggs, streaked with reddish-brown, incubated by female for about 45 days. Chicks fledge at 65–80 days.

LIFESTYLE: This extraordinary bird is unique: a bird of prey that hunts by striding over the ground on its extremely long legs. Some experts believe that it is more closely allied to the South American seriamas – long-legged ground birds that live in a similar way – and that its resemblance to birds of prey is coincidence. But there is no doubt that it is an expert hunter, able to subdue powerful venomous snakes and small mammals. It often hunts in pairs or family parties. It is attracted to grass fires, where it snatches up animals escaping from the flames and, after the blaze has

passed, searching the blackened ground for casualties. it usually roosts for the night on flat-topped acacia trees. Although it seldom flies while foraging, it can fly well and often soars on thermals like a vulture or stork.

HAWK ON STILTS
The storklike, scaly legs of the secretary bird raise its body beyond the reach of venomous snakes pinioned to the ground by its small but strong feet. It kills such prey by stamping on it.

OSPREY

Pandion haliaetus
Family: PANDIONIDAE
Order: FALCONIFORMES

DISTRIBUTION: Breeds on cliffs, in trees, or on ground, near fresh water or along coasts, across northern hemisphere from sub-Arctic to subtropics; also in Australia and adjacent parts of southeast Asia. Some birds migrate to warmer areas in winter.

SIZE: Length 22–23in (55–58cm); weight 2.7–4.2lb (1.2–1.9kg); female larger than male.

APPEARANCE: Resembles large, pale eagle with long wings. Dark brown above, white below, with white head and dark eye-stripe. Dark wrist patches on underwings; streaked band on breast, most prominent on female.

DIET: Mainly fish; also small mammals and insects.

BREEDING: Nests in spring, in large, untidy nest of sticks, bones, seaweed, and debris built on tree, crag, or artificial platform. Returns to same nest each year, adding more material so it reaches an immense size. 2–4 creamy or yellowish eggs, spotted and blotched with dark brown or chestnut-red. Incubated by both parents, especially the female, for 35–38 days. Chicks, cared for by both parents, fledge at 51–59 days.

LIFESTYLE: One of the most widespread and successful birds of prey, the osprey is a specialist fish-catcher. It is uniquely adapted for diving into the water and seizing its slippery, struggling prey, having waterproof plumage, nostrils that seal shut when it dives to prevent water being forced into its lungs, and long-clawed feet with spiny, fish-gripping pads beneath its toes.

When hunting, an osprey typically hovers over the water searching for fish, then descends in stages to check out any potential victims. When it locates a fish it plunges headlong with its wings half-folded, often submerging its body, and impales its prey on its talons. Then it struggles free of the water and flies off to a feeding perch, holding the fish head-first with one foot behind the other for streamlining.

Although ospreys disperse for the winter they return to the same nest sites year after year and meet up with their previous partners. They cement their bond with aerial chases, and the male makes dramatic dives and swoops, often

with a fish clasped in his talons.

Ospreys suffered badly from pesticide poisoning in the 1960s and 1970s, especially in North America and western Europe, but these birds have recovered well.

FEEDING PERCH
An osprey always takes its prey back to a favorite perch, and tears it apart with its long-hooked bill while gripping it with one of its specially adapted feet. It discards most of the bones.

SNAIL KITE

Rostrhamus sociabilis
Family: ACCIPITRIDAE
Order: ACCIPITRIFORMES

DISTRIBUTION: Freshwater marshes with open water, lakes, lagoons, rice fields, and other low-altitude wetlands, with rushes or other low vegetation in Florida and Cuba, and from eastern Mexico south to Argentina. Populations in southernmost parts of South American range migrate north for winter.

SIZE: Length 15–18in (39–45cm); weight 10.75–14.5oz (305–410g).

APPEARANCE: Smallish bird of prey with very long, slender hook to bill, large, broad wings and slightly notched tail. Male has black plumage, with broad white band at base of tail and narrower one at tail-tip; legs red. Female dark brown, with reddish edges to feathers of upperparts, heavily blotched with cream below, pale buff cheeks and stripe over eye; similar tail pattern to male's.

DIET: Aquatic apple snails; occasionally other, smaller water snails; also freshwater crabs in parts of Venezuela and Brazil.

BREEDING: Season varies. Forms small loose nesting colonies in vegetation or low shrubs (occasionally trees) growing in, over or next to water. Male builds nest, a bulky platform of twigs lined with finer plant material. 2–5 white eggs, speckled and spotted with various shades of brown or reddish-brown, with large blotches of same color; incubated by 26–28 days. Young fledge at 23–30 days.

LIFESTYLE: The snail kite is a highly specialized bird of prey that feeds almost exclusively on just one kind of water snail. It can survive only in continuously flooded habitats that provide sufficient prey. The snail kite scans its surroundings for snails both from perches and in slow, flapping flight on its big, paddle-shaped wings. After snatching the snail in one

foot, it deftly transfers it to its bill
in flight, then takes it to a favorite
feeding perch. Here, it uses the
long sickle-shaped upper mandible
of its bill to neatly sever the muscle
holding the snail's body in its shell
and extracts its fleshy prize.

PATIENT PERCHER
The snail kite spends a
great deal of time on a
low branch, fence post
or other perch, waiting
patiently until it spots
an apple snail to swoop
down upon and snatch.

NORTHERN SPARROWHAWK

Accipiter nisus
Family: ACCIPITRIDAE
Order: FALCONIFORMES

DISTRIBUTION: Breeds in Europe, Asia, and the northwestern tip of Africa; northern birds migrate south in winter as far as Persian Gulf and Southeast Asia. Favors wooded areas, parks, and gardens.

SIZE: Length 11–15in (28–38cm); weight 5.3–11.5oz (150–325g); female much bigger than male.

APPEARANCE: Long-tailed hawk with short, rounded wings. Male slatey-gray above, with dark bars on tail; pale underparts finely barred reddish-brown; rufous cheeks and flanks; orange eyes. Female darker gray-brown above, with underparts barred gray; white stripe above yellow eye. Yellow legs and base of bill.

DIET: Mainly small birds caught on the wing; also insects and small mammals such as voles and mice.

BREEDING: In spring. Nest built mainly by female, in a tree: a loose platform of twigs lined with leafy twigs. 2–7 bluish-white eggs, spotted, blotched, or streaked with dark brown, incubated by female for 32–35 days. Male brings food. Female broods chicks at first, then both parents feed them. Chicks fledge at 24–30 days, but stay with parents for a further month.

LIFESTYLE: The fast, agile northern sparrowhawk is specialized for hunting other birds in the confined spaces of the forest. Its relatively short wings and long tail give it the maneuvrability and compact profile it needs to jink and swerve through the trees in pursuit of prey. It takes its victims by surprise, often darting out from a perch or flying low in the lee of a hedge before bursting up to pluck a songbird from its perch. It carries its prey to a favorite "plucking post" to butcher it with its hooked bill, and these perches are often surrounded by feathers and the discarded remains of prey.

SIZE DIFFERENCE
Much smaller than his
mate, the male hunts
small tits and finches
while the female
targets bigger birds
such as thrushes.

In the open it has a low, fast flap-and-glide flight, but it may also soar high in the air. In spring males perform circling or switchback display flights over their breeding territories, and females join in soaring and diving displays.

Northern sparrowhawks were badly hit by pesticide poisoning in the 1960s, but have recovered since the most damaging chemicals were outlawed in much of Europe in the 1970s. But many are still shot by game wardens, often illegally.

BALD EAGLE

Haliaeetus leucocephalus
Family: ACCIPITRIDAE
Order: FALCONIFORMES

DISTRIBUTION: Breeds along sea coasts, large rivers, and lakes across much of North America; most northern populations winter farther south.

SIZE: Length 31–37in (79–94cm); weight 8–14lb (3.6–6.4kg).

APPEARANCE: Large, dark brown eagle; white head and tail, very large yellow bill, yellow, legs and eyes.

DIET: Mainly fish; also small mammals, birds, and carrion.

BREEDING: In late fall in south, spring in north. Pairs for life. Builds large, deep nest of branches and sticks, lined with grass, in tall tree, on cliff, or on small island. Nest is re-used, repaired, and added to annually. 1–3 white eggs, incubated by female for 34–39 days. Young cared for by female at first, male bringing food; then both parents bring food. Chicks fledge at 9–14 weeks, but parental care continues for another 4–6 weeks.

LIFESTYLE: The bald eagle is one of the fish eagles. Many of its relatives hunt almost exclusively at sea, but the bald eagle is more versatile. Although it favors fish, it catches a wide variety of live prey, steals food from other birds, and scavenges for carrion and scraps. This flexibility allows it to live in a wide range of habitats, from the rivers and lakes of Canada to the dry sagebrush of Arizona. Many migrate between the two, wintering in the south when the northern lakes freeze over.

Yet most of the 100,000 or so bald eagles in North America live on the Pacific coasts of Alaska and British Columbia, where fish are plentiful and accessible throughout the year. Here they enjoy an annual feast in the fall when thousands of Pacific salmon swim upriver to spawn, and then die. Hundreds of bald eagles gather to wade into the shallows and scoop the exhausted, dying salmon from the water.

AMERICAN EAGLE
Despite being adopted
as the national emblem
of the United States in
1782, the bald eagle is
still regularly shot by
illegal hunters, and
poisoned by farmers
who accuse it of
stealing lambs.

At the beginning of the breeding
season pairs perform spectacular
display flights, soaring high in the
air, locking talons and tumbling
from the sky. Since the birds return
to their old nest sites to breed,
they normally team up with their
partners from the previous season,
and the aerial displays help them
get re-acquainted.

Although badly hit by hunting and
pesticide poisoning in the past, the
bald eagle is now protected and
increasing throughout its range.

GOLDEN EAGLE

Aquila chrysaetos
Family: ACCIPITRIDAE
Order: FALCONIFORMES

DISTRIBUTION: Breeds throughout much of North America, Europe, North Africa, the Middle East, and Asia, outside the tropics. Many northern populations migrate south in winter, but some are resident.

SIZE: Length 30–39in (76–99cm); weight 7.7–10.8lb (3.5–4.9kg).

APPEARANCE: A large, powerful brown eagle with a golden or tawny tinge over its crown and nape, a square, faintly barred tail, and feathered legs. Large, yellowish-black bill with yellow skin at base; brown eyes; yellow legs.

DIET: Mainly small mammals up to size of small deer; also birds from larks to grouse and geese. Eats a lot of carrion in winter.

BREEDING: Breeds in late winter in south, spring to summer in north. Builds large nest of branches and twigs, lined with leafy twigs, grasses, or conifer needles, in tree or on cliff or high rock. Adds to nest annually, so it can grow to immense size. 1–3 white eggs, often spotted or blotched with brown, chestnut, and pale gray, incubated usually by female for 43–45 days. Chick brooded by female at first, then fed by both parents. Usually only one chick survives to fledge at 63–70 days.

LIFESTYLE: The magnificent and graceful golden eagle is a bird of remote wilderness regions – mainly mountains and bleak moorlands, but also lowland forests and wetlands. It hunts by patrolling a huge range at low altitude, watching the ground for prey and pouncing on its victims in fast, slanting dives. It spends many hours on the wing, soaring high into the sky on updrafts, gliding across country, wheeling, swooping, and climbing. It achieves many of these maneuvers without beating its wings at all, but uses deep, slow wingbeats when necessary.

AERIAL DISPLAYS
Breeding golden eagles perform breathtaking aerial displays, soaring over their territory, plunging to earth with their wings folded back, then climbing to repeat the performance.

Golden eagles pair for life, and in areas where they are resident, such as Scotland, they stay on the same territory throughout the year. Pairs often feed together, and even cooperate to catch prey. They use the same nest for breeding each season, but may abandon it if they are disturbed. This has made the eagles scarce in many parts of their range, even where they are protected from persecution.

COMMON KESTREL

Falco tinnunculus
Family: FALCONIDAE
Order: FALCONIFORMES

DISTRIBUTION: Breeds on open moorland, farmland, savanna, suburbs, and towns through most of Africa, Europe and Asia, except the far north. Northern populations migrate south in winter.

SIZE: Length 12–14in (31–35cm); weight 4.1–10.6oz (117–299g).

APPEARANCE: Typical falcon with long, pointed wings and long tail. Male chestnut with darker spots and black tail bar; head and tail bluish-gray; buff below. Female and juvenile chestnut overall above, with black bars, and no gray. Both sexes have dark wingtips, dark "mustache" stripe below the eye, yellow legs, yellowish hooked bill with dark tip, and yellow eyes.

DIET: Mainly voles, mice, and other small mammals; also birds, lizards, frogs, insects, and earthworms.

BREEDING: Mates in late winter to spring. Lays eggs in unlined tree hollow or rock crevice, on rocky ledge, or in abandoned nest of another bird such as a crow. Lays 4–9 white or yellowish-buff eggs, speckled dark reddish-brown, incubated mainly by female for 27–29 days. Chicks brooded and fed by female, with male bringing food; fledge at 27–39 days.

LIFESTYLE: One of the world's most versatile and abundant birds of prey, the common kestrel is also one of the most distinctive. It has perfected the art of searching for small animals by hovering in mid-air, usually about 30 feet (10m) above the ground. Its tail flared and wings quivering, it makes constant adjustments to keep its head perfectly still, watching intently for the slightest movement. It may hover for several minutes like this, then sideslip away to try another spot. It often hunts over grassy roadsides, where small rodents are common, and is frequently seen along busy highways. In hill country it hangs in updrafts, barely moving its wings, showing a mastery of the air that few other birds can match. When it sees a victim it drops to snatch it up in its talons, then carries it away to a favorite perch to tear apart.

Despite its refined hovering skills, the common kestrel is no specialist. It can take a wide variety of prey, enabling it to thrive in all kinds of habitats. It is tolerant of human neighbors, and this allows it to breed on farmland and even in city centers. The pairs perform dramatic courtship displays, circling and chasing each other, the male diving on the female in mock attacks. The common kestrel is probably the most familiar bird of prey in Europe.

VANTAGE POINT
Famous for its hovering hunting technique, this kestrel often hunts from a perch, swooping down to seize animals on the ground or small birds in mid-air.

PEREGRINE FALCON

Falco peregrinus
Family: FALCONIDAE
Order: FALCONIFORMES

DISTRIBUTION: Open country and coasts worldwide, except polar regions, deserts, and some islands.

SIZE: Length 14–19in (36–48cm); weight 1.3–2.1lb (611–952g); female much larger than male.

APPEARANCE: Powerfully-built falcon with long, pointed wings, tapering tail, and feathered legs. Dark grayish-blue above, with whitish to reddish-buff underparts heavily barred with black; dark "mustache" extends around eye; white chin and cheeks. Legs, bill-base, and bare skin around eye yellow; bill dark gray. Male darker than female.

DIET: Mainly birds, caught in flight; also some mammals.

BREEDING: Breeds in spring and summer, season varying throughout global range. Lays eggs in unlined hollow on cliff ledge, high crag, or building. 2–6 creamy or buff eggs, heavily marked with chestnut or red, gray, and purple, incubated by both parents for 31–38 days. Chicks fledge at 45 days.

LIFESTYLE: The peregrine is the fastest and most spectacular of the bird-killing falcons. Big and powerful – especially the female – it has the strength to kill a bird as big as a duck or a curlew, although most of its victims are the size of pigeons or crows. It patrols high in the air or watches from a high vantage point, and when it sees a suitable victim it typically plunges from the sky on half-closed wings, at speeds of 100mph (160 kmh) or more. It rips into its prey with its hooklike rear talon, often killing it on impact, then follows it down as its tumbles from the sky. If its victim is still alive it kills it by severing the spinal cord with its bill, then usually plucks and eats its meal where it fell.

Like many birds of prey, peregrine pairs perform spectacular aerial courtship displays, circling high into the air and plummeting down again while calling with harsh chattering cries. Today they typically breed in remote wilderness regions, but they are surprisingly adaptable; some pairs regularly nest on tall chimneys and high-rise buildings, even in city centers.

Peregrines are on the increase throughout much of their range, but they were once heavily persecuted. Many were shot because they were viewed as a danger to valuable gamebirds, and in World War II the peregrine population of southern England was eliminated to remove any threat to carrier pigeons bringing messages from occupied Europe. In the 1960s huge numbers were wiped out by pesticide poisoning.

SUPERSENSE
The peregrine can spot its prey from far away thanks to its superb eyesight, which magnifies the image like a pair of binoculars and has extra-fine definition.

BARN OWL

Tyto alba
Family: TYTONIDAE
Order: STRIGIFORMES

DISTRIBUTION: Open country with scattered trees over much of the world, from the United States to the Strait of Magellan near the southern tip of South America; from western Europe to the Black Sea; through Middle East to southern Asia; Africa apart from the Sahara; and Australia.

SIZE: Length 12–17in (30–44cm); weight 7–25oz (200–700g).

APPEARANCE: A pale owl with a large head, a flat, heart-shaped face, dark eyes, and long legs. Plumage reddish gold to rusty-brown above, mottled with gray and buff; underparts, leg feathers, and face white; underwings pale; feet brown; bill yellowish to buffish.

DIET: Mainly rodents taken from ground; also other small mammals, large insects, and birds.

BREEDING: Nests in late winter or spring, in tree hollow, rock crevice, haystack, or old building. 3–11 white eggs, incubated by female for 32–34 days. Chicks cared for by both parents; fledge at 60 days.

LIFESTYLE: Like most owls, the barn owl is specialized for hunting small mammals by night. Its superb hearing is especially sensitive to the rustles and squeaks of voles, mice, and other rodents in the grass, and the soft edges of its flight feathers act as "silencers," enabling it to track its prey by ear and pounce on it without warning. It prefers to hunt on the wing, patrolling low over the ground with a light, buoyant flight action, and occasionally hovering to check up on a possible target. When it pinpoints a victim it plunges down head-first, then swings its long legs forward to seize its prey in its powerful talons. Experiments in darkened rooms have proved that a barn owl can catch a mouse by sound alone, in total darkness when it can see nothing at all.

The barn owl's skill at catching vermin made it a valuable ally for farmers in the past, when grain was kept in barns. Its preference for nesting in such buildings was encouraged, and this was probably a factor in its success. But today many traditional farm buildings have been demolished, and the use of pesticides has made mice and other rodents much less common. So in many parts of its range – and particularly in North America and Europe – the barn owl is in decline, and its eerie, screeching call is becoming rarer each year.

BLACK EYES
The heart-shaped face and relatively small, dark eyes of the barn owl mark it out from the typical owls of the family Strigidae, which tend to have rounder faces and bigger, more colorful eyes.

SNOWY OWL

Nyctea scandiaca
Family: STRIGIDAE
Order: STRIGIFORMES

DISTRIBUTION: Breeds throughout the Arctic region, on tundra and moorlands; may winter farther south, as far as the temperate zone, around coasts, marshes, sand dunes, and pastures.

SIZE: Length 21–26in (53–66cm); weight 3.6–6.5lb (1.6–2.9kg); female larger than male.

APPEARANCE: Male is large snow-white owl with brownish bars and spots near tips of feathers on wings and tail; underparts faintly barred with very pale brown. Female has much heavier, darker bars and spots. Legs and feet heavily feathered. Blackish-brown bill; yellow eyes.

DIET: Mainly lemmings, voles, and medium-sized birds; also hares and other small mammals.

BREEDING: Female makes a scrape on the ground in spring, among mosses or stones, sometimes lined with moss and feathers. 4–10 white eggs, depending on abundance of prey, incubated by female for 32–37 days. Young brooded by female at first; male brings food. Chicks leave nest after 2.5–3.5 weeks, and fledge at 8–9 weeks.

WHITE DISPLAY
The almost pure white plumage of the male snowy owl is probably more for show than camouflage, since the barred female is harder to see on the almost snow-free nest site in summer.

LIFESTYLE: Insulated against the cold by its thick plumage and feathered feet, the snowy owl may spend all year hunting on the icy tundra of the high Arctic. In summer it hunts largely by sight in the 24-hour daylight, and often perches on rocks or other vantage points to survey its surroundings for prey. In the darkness of winter it relies on its ears to detect lemmings scurrying through their runs under the snow. Lemmings are its main prey, and notoriously their populations often soar to plague proportions. Snowy owls make the most of these booms by laying extra-large clutches of eggs, and rearing as many young as possible. But the lemming booms are often followed by population crashes, and then the owls scatter across the tundra – and often far to the south – to catch what prey they can find. Many may die, but their numbers are made up when the survivors raise large families during the next lemming boom.

TAWNY OWL

Strix aluco
Family: STRIGIDAE
Order: STRIGIFORMES

DISTRIBUTION: Open woodland, parks, and large gardens across Europe, northwest Africa and parts of Asia to southern China up to 9,000ft (2,750m).

SIZE: Length 14–15in (37–39cm); weight 13.5–22oz (385–620g).

APPEARANCE: Bulky, medium-sized brown owl with pale or rufous facial disk, pale greenish-yellow bill, and bluish-black eyes. Upperparts reddish-brown, mottled and streaked with dark brown; white patches and dark bars on wings; barred tail. Underparts buff, with darker streaks and faint bars; feathered legs. Sexes alike.

DIET: Mainly rodents and small birds, plus frogs and insects.

BREEDING: Nests in spring, using a shallow unlined depression in a tree hole or rock crevice, or abandoned nest of another bird; sometimes on a building or in a nestbox. 1–7 white eggs, incubated by female for 28–30 days. Chicks fledge at 32–37 days.

LIFESTYLE: The strictly nocturnal tawny owl roosts in tree by day, emerging to hunt at dusk. It occupies the same woodland territory throughout the year, so it knows all the best places to find prey at different seasons. Rather than waste energy flying about, it finds a good perch and settles to wait. It has extremely good night vision and acute hearing, allowing it to pinpoint victims on starless nights that, to us, seem completely black. Its soft-edged flight feathers make no noise as it swoops down for the kill, enabling it to stay on target and giving its prey no warning. The owl snatches it up in its talons, carries it back to the perch, and swallows it whole.

In spring, unmated males attract females with breathy, quavering hoots. The females often reply with their sharp "ke-wick" contact calls,

and the duet between the two was once thought to come from one bird: the classic "tu-whit, tu-woo" owl call of many stories.

Although essentially woodland birds, tawny owls are very adaptable and often breed in city parks. They can be fiercely defensive of their nest sites, and have been known to swoop down on people who have unknowingly walked too close and slash at them with their talons.

THREAT DISPLAY
A cornered tawny owl will attempt to scare off its enemy with an intimidating display, gaping its hooked bill and fanning its wings to make itself look bigger and more dangerous.

EURASIAN SWIFT

Apus apus
Family: APODIDAE
Order: APODIFORMES

DISTRIBUTION: Breeds throughout Europe, northwest Africa, and parts of Central Asia and the Far East. Migrates south to spend the northern winter in Africa.

SIZE: Length 6.5in (16–17cm); weight 1.1–1.5oz (31–43g).

APPEARANCE: Sleek, fast-flying, with long, curved, tapering wings and short forked tail. Plumage dark grayish-black all over, with whitish throat; legs and bill blackish; eyes dark brown. Sexes alike.

DIET: Small flying insects and airborne spiders.

BREEDING: Nests in colonies under eaves or roofs of buildings, in rock crevices or woodpecker holes, in late spring and summer. Shallow cup-shaped nest of plant material and feathers, collected from the air and glued together with saliva. 2–4 white eggs, incubated by female for 14–20 days. Chicks fed by both parents. Fledge at 5–9 weeks.

LIFESTYLE: All swifts are highly aerial birds, but the Eurasian swift must hold the record for nonstop flight. From the day it leaves the nest where it hatched, to the day it lands at its own breeding site, it probably spends all its time on the wing. Since it may remain for two or three years hunting in Africa before returning north to breed, it could easily spend over three years in the air without once landing.

It can live like this because it gets almost everything it needs from the air. It feeds only on small airborne insects and infant spiders that float through the air on threads of gossamer. To drink, it swoops over a pool to scoop up a mouthful of water. It can even sleep on the wing, rising high in the sky and circling with slow, instinctive wingbeats and short glides.

The only thing that the air cannot supply is a nesting site. Today most Eurasian swifts nest in the roof spaces of buildings, gathering

HIGH PASSION
Eurasian swifts are so aerial by nature that they may even mate on the wing, locked together in a fluttering glide. More commonly they mate on the nest that they have built together from fragments of airborne debris.

in traditional colonies every spring. They chase each other around the rooftops with shrieking cries, and mated pairs gather nesting material and, eventually, food for their young. If the weather is bad insect prey may be hard to find, but the young can survive without food for several days by becoming torpid. Normally the long days of the northern summer allow them to find enough, and by August the adults and young are ready to abandon their nests and fly away to Africa.

RIVER KINGFISHER

Alcedo atthis
Family: ALCEDINIDAE
Order: CORACIIFORMES

DISTRIBUTION: By fresh water from Baltic states, western Europe, and North Africa to central and southeast Asia and the southwest Pacific. Northern birds winter farther south, often along coasts.

SIZE: Length 6in (16–17cm); weight 0.8–1.2oz (23–33g).

APPEARANCE: Vividly-colored bird with short, stumpy body, short tail, large head, and long, flattened, pointed bill. Upper parts iridescent cobalt blue to emerald green, with electric blue on back and rump; underparts light chestnut. Wide chestnut stripe from bill through eye; white throat. Short red legs; black bill, reddish at base in female; dark brown eyes.

DIET: Mainly small freshwater fish; also aquatic insects, amphibians, crustaceans, and mollusks.

BREEDING: In spring. Pair make tunnel up to 39in (1m) long, in bank near water, with round nest chamber up to 6in (15cm) across. No nest material, but chamber becomes lined with fish bones. 4–8 white eggs, incubated by both parents for 19–21 days. Chicks fledge at 23–27 days.

LIFESTYLE: Usually seen as an electric blue streak shooting low over the water on whirring wings, often giving its shrill "cheeee" call, the river kingfisher can be surprisingly hard to locate when it is perched quietly watching for prey. It may wait patiently for a long time, almost motionless, although it also hovers over the water if there is no convenient perch. When it sees a potential meal it flies down in a power dive, plunging beneath the surface to seize its victim in its long bill, then surges out of the water to fly back to its perch with its prey.

Aggressively territorial, it defends a long stretch of river or stream against rivals, and a male may even drive away its own mate in winter. If the water of its home stream freezes over it may have to move to larger lakes, floodwaters, or even the coast, but if possible the adult males defend their breeding territories throughout the year. In spring the pairs perform noisy chasing displays in the air near a potential nest site, then get to work on the nest tunnel with their bills. Both parents bring fish and other food for the young, flying straight into the burrow without hesitation. Each young bird needs up to 18 small fish a day.

KNOCKOUT
After returning to its perch with its prey the kingfisher beats it against the wood to subdue it, before flipping it around to swallow it head-first. The red on this bird's bill identifies it as a female.

LAUGHING KOOKABURRA

Dacelo novaeguineae
Family: ALCEDINIDAE
Order: CORACIIFORMES

DISTRIBUTION: In dry, open forest, farmland with trees, city parks and gardens native to east and southeast Australia; introduced to southwest Australia, Kangaroo and Flinders Islands, Tasmania and New Zealand.

SIZE: Length 15.5–16.5in (39–42cm); weight 11–17oz (310–480g).

APPEARANCE: Stocky, with short neck, large head with stout, pointed bill. Upperparts blackish-brown mottled with pale blue on shoulders and rump; white patch in outer wing; tail reddish-cinnamon, barred black, and with white edges and tip. Underparts and head whitish, latter with blackish-brown streaks on top of crown and dark brown eyestripe; legs and feet pale greenish; bill with blackish upper mandible and horn-coloured lower mandible below; eyes dark brown.

DIET: Snakes, lizards, rodents, small adult and nestling birds and birds' eggs, fish, crayfish, insects, earthworms, spiders and other invertebrates, scraps of food from garbage dumps and bird feeders.

BREEDING: September to January in native range. Nests in holes in trees, termite nests in trees, banks, nestboxes. 1–4 white eggs, incubated for 24–26 days. Chicks fledge at 33-39 days, but depend on parents and "helpers" for food for at least two months.

LIFESTYLE: Despite the family name, most kingfisher species, including this kookaburra, do not specialize in catching fish, and can live far from water. One of the main reasons for the laughing kookaburra's success is that is an adaptable bird that can feed on a very wide range of prey. Snakes are often an important part of the diet. The kookaburra kills large

OFTEN HEARD AND SEEN
One of the best-known of all Australian birds, it is a common species that has benefited from human settlement.

ones by dropping them from a height or battering them on a branch. They also visit bird feeders, where they are particularly fond of cheese and raw meat. Kookaburras pair for life, and a pair remains year-round on its territory, usually with a band of "helpers"– up to five well-grown offspring. All work together to defend the territory against rivals, and advertise their ownership by the famous loud, laughing song. This performance, in which the birds cock their tails as they laugh, is heard mainly at dawn and dusk. The helpers also assist the nesting pair in incubating the eggs and feeding and brooding the chicks. They may help for up to four years before finding their own mates and moving away or replacing parents that have died.

EUROPEAN NIGHTJAR

Caprimulgus europaeus
Family: CAPRIMULGIDAE
Order: CAPRIMULGIFORMES

DISTRIBUTION: Breeds in open woodlands, heaths, and deserts throughout Europe, southern Scandinavia, and Asia as far east as Afghanistan and Lake Baikal. Winters in Africa south of the Sahara. Many of its favored habitats has been swept away or built over (and insecticides have also destroyed much of its prey), so the strange song of the European nightjar is becoming increasingly rare in many parts of its former range.

SIZE: Length 11in (28cm); weight 2.6–3.5oz (75–100g).

APPEARANCE: Long-bodied, short-legged, with small, flattened head, short bill, long wings and tail. Plumage cryptic grayish-brown, spotted and barred with tawny and dark brown. Male has white patches on tips of its wings and outer tail feathers, visible in flight.

DIET: Moths, beetles, and other night-flying insects.

BREEDING: Lays eggs in a shallow scrape on the ground, usually among dead leaves and twigs, in late spring and summer. Usually 2 creamy to grayish-white eggs, spotted or streaked with yellowish-brown or dark brown; incubated by female in daytime, male at night, for 18 days. Chicks reared by both parents; fledge at 16–18 days; independent at 31–34 days. Female may start second brood while male looks after first one.

LIFESTYLE: It hunts its insect prey like a night-flying swallow, wheeling and darting through the gloom to snatch its victims out of the air. Although its bill is small it has a huge gape, fringed with stiff sensory bristles to make sure of every catch. It hunts by sight, and is most active at twilight or on moonlit nights. By day it roosts on the ground or lying along a branch, concealed by its astonishingly effective camouflage.

AIR FREIGHT

Nightjars were believed to carry their eggs in their bills to remove them from danger. Although a nightjar's enormous gape may be big enough for the job the story is regarded as a myth.

The nightjar is named for the male's weird mechanical song – a long, soft, rising-and-falling "churr" that sounds rather like a small motor in the distance. He may sing for hours on end with only brief pauses. He also has wing-clapping display flight, during which he flashes the white patches on his wingtips and tail. These act as recognition markings, allowing a female to pick him out and identify him in the dim light.

EUROPEAN BEE-EATER

> *Merops apiaster*
> Family: MEROPIDAE
> Order: CORACIIFORMES

DISTRIBUTION: Breeds in open country, cultivated land, scrub, and woodland, often near rivers, from southern Europe and northwest Africa across the Middle East and Asia to northern India, and in South Africa. Winters in Africa.

SIZE: Length 10–10.5in (25–27cm); weight 2oz (56.6g).

APPEARANCE: Brilliantly colored bird with pointed wings, down-curved bill, square tail with long central feathers, and small feet with partly-joined toes. Bluish-green with chestnut head and mantle, shading to golden yellow on back. Yellow throat with thick black border blending into a distinct black eyestripe. Blackish-gray legs and bill; brown eyes.

DIET: Bees and wasps, plus dragonflies and other flying insects.

BREEDING: Nests in large colonies in spring and summer. Each pair excavates a tunnel, up to 9 feet (2.7m) long, into a bank, sloping down to a round, unlined nest chamber, soon lined with insect remains. 4–10 white eggs, incubated by both parents for 20 days. Chicks, cared for by both parents, fledge at 20–25 days.

LIFESTYLE: The exquisitely colored European bee-eater is a common sight on warm, sunny riversides in southern Europe, where it often perches on dead trees and overhead wires in small flocks. At intervals small groups fly off like swallows, or soar away on rising thermal air currents in search of prey, staying in contact with their mellow, liquid, musical calls.

Bee-eaters really do eat bees, as well as wasps and other large airborne insects, which they snatch out of the air during fast swoops and glides, or by sallying up from their perches. They seem to have some immunity to bee and wasp

stings, but they take care to kill each victim before wiping its tail end against a perch to squeeze out the venom. A bee-eater is smart enough to know the difference between a stinging wasp and a striped, yet harmless hoverfly, which it swallows straight away.

Bee-eater nesting colonies are busy, colorful places, with birds continually flying in and out of the nesting burrows as they bring food for their young. If a dangerous, bird-hunting predator such as a falcon appears, the bee-eaters will often gang up to drive it away, and they have been seen attacking burrow-hunting ermines by diving at their heads. They attract birdwatchers and in some places the constant traffic of people disturbs colonies. A more serious threat is the relentless conversion of small, mixed farms into large cereal fields, regularly sprayed with pesticides.

AIR STRIKE
The long, pointed bill of a European bee-eater is ideal for seizing big flying insects in the air, allowing the bird to get a good grip on its victim's body while avoiding its whirring wings.

HOOPOE

Upupa epops
Family: UPUPIDAE
Order: CORACIIFORMES

DISTRIBUTION: Breeds in woodlands, orchards, olive groves, vineyards, parkland, steppe (Asia), dry savanna (Africa and Madagascar) across much of Europe (except in north), central and southern Asia and Africa. Northern birds migrate to winter farther south, in open country.

SIZE: Length 10–12.5in (26–32cm); weight 1.7–3oz (48–85g).

APPEARANCE: Unmistakable thrush-sized bird having long, slim, tapering, slightly downcurved bill and large crest with barred edge, erected when excited; head, most of crest and body pinkish-brown; wings heavily barred black-and-white; belly and rump white; tail black with white band; bill and legs gray; eyes brown.

DIET: Mainly large insects and their larvae, including crickets, locusts, beetles, and caterpillars; also small vertebrates, such as lizards, snakes and frogs.

BREEDING: Varies according to locality. Nests in hole in tree, tree stump, wall of old building, cliff, or among rocks, sometimes in nest boxes. 4–8 gray, pale yellow or olive eggs, incubated by female for 16–18 days; male brings food. Chicks reared by both parents; fledge at 24–32 days. Often raises two broods in south of range.

LIFESTYLE: The boldly patterned hoopoe is a familiar bird throughout its range, living alongside humans around villages and traditionally managed farmland. Its requirements are areas of short grass or soft soil where it can feed, and scattered trees or other sites where it can find nesting holes.

Hoopoes are often seen probing and digging for insect prey with their long bills into soft ground, also among leaf-litter, garbage, and dried-out animal dung. The birds are not usually sociable, feeding mainly on their own or in pairs,

SUNBATHING
A hoopoe may flatten itself,
its bill pointing skywards: this
may hide the bird from
predators, but is more likely
to be a form of sunbathing.

which breed apart from others and defend a territory around the nest hole. The birds communicate their mood to one another by adjusting the position of the prominent crest: it is lowered when they are relaxed, and raised and fanned when they are alarmed or excited.

Both the common and scientific names refer to the lovely, mellow hooting "hoop-hoop-hoop" spring song of the male. Despite its bold plumage, the hoopoe can be hard to see on the ground, but when it takes wing, flying off with floppy wingbeats like a huge butterfly, the black-and-white wings are very noticeable.

115

NORTHERN FLICKER

Colaptes auratus
Family: PICIDAE
Order: PICIFORMES

DISTRIBUTION: Open woodlands, forest edges, farmland, parks, gardens and other open country throughout North and Central America, from the far north of Alaska and Canada south to Nicaragua. Northern populations, breeding in Canada and extreme northern USA, winter farther south.

SIZE: Length 10–14in (25.5–36cm); weight 3.2–5.9oz (92–167g).

APPEARANCE: Medium-sized woodpecker; upperparts brown, barred blackish; underparts paler, spotted blackish, with black crescent on breast; rump white, conspicuous in flight, tail black; underwing and head plumage varies between geographic races; two distinct groups occur in North America, "yellow-shafted flickers" in north and east, with underwings and most of undertail yellow, gray crown and hind neck with red crescent on nape, buff face, and black mustache in male; and "red-shafted flickers" in west and Mexico, with reddish underwings and undertail, brown crown and hind neck without red crescent, gray face, and red mustache in male; legs gray; bill black; eyes deep brown.

DIET: Mainly ants; also other insects, and many fruits, berries, seeds in winter.

BREEDING: February to July overall, varies geographically; both sexes may chisel out nest-hole with bills in dead wood of tree, or a wide range of other sites; often use old cavity instead; 3–12 white eggs, incubated for 11–12 days by both sexes, male taking greater share. Chicks cared for by both parents. Fledge at 25–28 days.

LIFESTYLE: This is the most terrestrial of all North American woodpeckers. With its slender bill and mainly ground-feeding habits, the northern flicker may not be

MAKING A POINT
This male yellow-shafted
northern flicker is
threatening a rival by
angling its sharp bill and
spreading its wings and
tail; an attack may follow.

recognized by many people as a
woodpecker. It hops about in
places such as lawns, roadsides,
and woodland floors in search of
food. It uses its spike of a bill to
sweep aside leaves to expose
insect prey, from termites to
caterpillars and aphids, and hack
into the nests of ants, which form
up to 75 percent of its diet. It also
feeds in trees like most of its
relatives, and visits bird feeders.
Prey is usually licked up with the

barbed, sticky tip of the bird's
remarkably long tongue

Flickers may use a wide range of
nest sites, from fenceposts and
bird boxes to wooden house roofs.
One or more pairs even tried to
excavate a nest hole in the Space
Shuttle *Discovery*.

GREEN WOODPECKER

Picus viridus
Family: PICIDAE
Order: PICIFORMES

DISTRIBUTION: In woodlands, forests, parks and gardens from southern Scandinavia, the British Isles (excluding Ireland), western Europe, and North Africa to western Russia, Turkey, Iran, and the Caspian Sea.

SIZE: Length 12in (30cm); weight 5.3–7oz (150–200g).

APPEARANCE: Big, long-bodied, long-billed woodpecker. Upper parts green with yellow rump, conspicuous in flight; underparts paler. Red crown and nape; wide black eyestripe. Male has red, black-edged mustache, female has all-black mustache. Dark gray legs and bill.

DIET: Mainly ants taken from nests on ground, plus insect larvae and spiders from bark; also berries and seeds. Sometimes raids beehives.

BREEDING: In spring the birds drill a hole in a tree, about 15in (38cm) deep. Nest cavity is unlined.

4–9 white eggs, incubated by both parents for 18–19 days. Chicks, cared for by both parents, fledge at 18–21 days.

LIFESTYLE: Woodpeckers are famous for their ability to hack into timber with their sharp bills, and many specialize in using this method to find wood-boring insect grubs. But the green woodpecker has developed a different skill. It feeds largely on ants, and is often seen foraging in the grass far from trees. It hops rather clumsily over the ground searching for ants and their nests, and often checking for danger. If alarmed it flies off with a low, fast, undulating flap-and-glide action, calling with a loud "kyu-kyu-kyu." In parts of Britain it is also known as the yaffle – a reference to its ringing, laughing, musical song.

Although solitary outside the breeding season, the birds form longterm pair bonds that may last for life. They get reacquainted in spring, with the courting male feeding the female after calling and displaying. They occupy a joint territory for the summer, then drift apart in the fall.

ANTEATER
The green woodpecker has an extremely long, sticky tongue that it uses to penetrate the narrow passages of ants' nests. Its bill is relatively weak, so it must excavate its nest holes in soft wood.

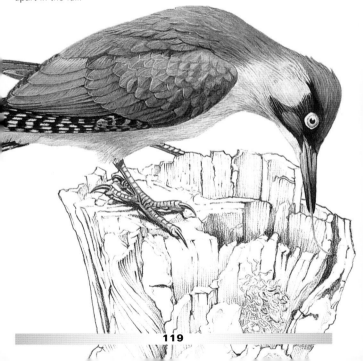

OSTRICH

Struthio camelus
Family: STRUTHIONIDAE
Order: STRUTHIONIFORMES

DISTRIBUTION: Semidesert and dry savanna grassland of west, east, and south Africa.

SIZE: Height 5.7–9ft (1.75–2.75m); weight 220–330lb (100–150kg); male larger than female.

APPEARANCE: Long neck, powerful legs, soft plumage, bare skin on head, neck, and thighs. Male black with white wing primaries; tail varies from whitish to gray, or cinnamon-brown; skin of head and neck pink or blue (depending on race) flushing bright red during courtship; brown eyes with large eyelashes. Female pale brown, with pinkish neck and head; wing tips sometimes whitish.

DIET: Plant shoots, leaves, flowers, and seeds.

BREEDING: Season varies with latitude. Male makes a number of unlined scrapes on ground. Female selects one and lays up to 12 large yellowish-white eggs, then several other females lay more eggs in the same scrape. The nest may initially contain up to 40 eggs; they are incubated by the male at night, and by the dominant female by day, for 42 days. Such a breeding arrangement, where the dominant female helps the male incubate the eggs of other females, is almost

unique. Perhaps her own eggs benefit from being part of a large clutch, but if there are too many eggs she has no scruples about ejecting eggs that are not her own. Exactly how she tells which eggs are which is still not clear. Chicks leave nest soon after hatching. They often gather together from several nests to form crèches, defended by one or two adults.

LIFESTYLE: The biggest and heaviest of all living birds, the magnificent ostrich is widely distributed throughout the drier parts of Africa – although it is much rarer than it used to be, owing to habitat destruction and hunting.

It is ideally adapted for life on arid grasslands, where its long stride allows it to gather sparse food from a wide area. It can tolerate losing up to a quarter of its body weight through dehydration, which gives it a big advantage in desert regions where sources of water are few and far between. It cannot fly, but it compensates for this with powerful legs that allow it to outrun most of its enemies. It can also keep walking indefinitely without becoming tired.

Ostriches rove in flocks of 10–50 in search of food. The big, black-and-white males defend their territories with loud, deep calls that resemble the roars of lions, and inflate the red-flushed skin of their necks in display. They also flourish their wing plumes, both to discourage their rivals and attract females. The smaller females also use their wings in display.

FASTEST THING ON TWO LEGS
The ostrich's big eyes enable it to see approaching danger, and its long, muscular legs give it the speed to makes its escape.

LESSER RHEA

Rhea pennata
Family: RHEIDAE
Order: RHEIFORMES

DISTRIBUTION: South America, in parts of Peru, Bolivia, Argentina and Chile. The two northern races (sometimes called the puna rhea) live in scrublands, bogs, heath and salt plains and grassy steppes of the Andes mountains, at 4,900–14,750 feet (1,500–4,500m). The southern race (sometimes called Darwin's rhea) inhabits Patagonia grassland and shrubby steppe up to 4,900 feet (1,500m).

SIZE: Length 37–39in (93–100cm); weight 33–55lb (15–25kg); female slightly smaller than male.

APPEARANCE: Huge, flightless bird with small head, long neck, bulky body and long legs with three-toed feet adapted for fast running. Plumage smooth, soft and brown (grayer in northern races), with white spots and fringes on upperparts (fewer in northern races and females). Juveniles lack white.

DIET: Mainly seeds, leaves, fruits, roots of a great variety of plants; also insects and some small vertebrates, such as lizards.

BREEDING: From September to January in the north, July to November in the south. The male fights rivals to acquire a harem of females. He makes a scrape on the ground, about 3.3 feet (1m) across, thinly lined with plant material. Several hens each take turns to lay their yellowish-green eggs in it, until it contains a total of up to 50. These are incubated by the male for about 40 days. Chicks, well developed on hatching, are led from nest by the male when a few days old. They are then cared for by the male for about six months.

LIFESTYLE: Rheas are gregarious birds, typically found in loose flocks of 5–30 outside the breeding season. Males become highly territorial in the breeding season. When running to escape dogs or other enemies, a rhea raises one wing and lowers the other, which enables it to make quick changes of direction. The northern races have been brought close to extinction, due to hunting for meat, skins and feathers and the taking of eggs; only a few hundred individuals survive. The southern race is more numerous, but also at risk, chiefly from the conversion of habitat to cattle pasture or croplands.

PROTECTIVE FATHER
Male rheas are model fathers, guarding their large brood, constantly on the lookout for danger. They fight fiercely to defend them, even attacking gauchos (cowboys) on horseback.

ONE-WATTLED CASSOWARY

Casuarius unappendiculatus
Family: CASUARIIDAE
Order: STRUTHIONIFORMES

New Guinea

DISTRIBUTION: Lowland rain forests and swamp forests of northern New Guinea.

SIZE: Length 1.2–1.5m (3.9–4.9ft); weight of males probably up to about 46lb (25kg), of females, probably up to 110lb (50kg).

APPEARANCE: Huge flightless bird with massive body, small wings, powerful legs and feet with only three large toes. Hard, coarse, glossy black plumage, with bare blue skin on head (often with reddish mark on back of crown), forming two folds at base of bill, abruptly changing to red, sometimes yellow, skin on lower neck, with a further one or two folds, and a red or yellow stripe running toward shoulder; flattened, horny, grayish to greenish "casque" or "helmet" on top of head; legs grayish-black; bill horn-colored; eyes yellowish. Immatures have dull brown plumage, lack bright skin colours on head and neck, and have smaller casque and wattles.

DIET: Fruit, seeds, and other plant material; small animals.

BREEDING: June-October. Nest a shallow scrape on forest floor, lined with grass and leaves. 3–8 pale to dark green eggs, incubated by male for 49–56 days. Chicks reared by male; leave nest soon after hatching.

LIFESTYLE: Along with the two other cassowary species, this impressive bird is potentially one the world's most dangerous. If it or its young are threatened by a dog or human for instance, it may leap up and lash out with its 4-inch (10-cm) long razor-sharp claw of the inner toe.

This can disembowel an opponent. However, cassowaries are far more at risk from humans than vice versa as a result of hunting and the destruction and fragmentation of the rain forests.

ELUSIVE FOREST-DWELLERS
Cassowaries are usually shy, retiring, and rarely seen; signs of their presence are the three-toed footprints and large piles of droppings.

EMU

Dromaius novaehollandiae
Family: DROMAIIDAE
Order: CASUARIFORMES

DISTRIBUTION: Throughout most of mainland Australia, except in driest deserts, dense forests, and urban areas. Nomadic.

SIZE: Height 6ft (1.8m); weight 110lb (50kg); females heavier than males.

APPEARANCE: Large, long-legged flightless bird with very small wings and long, loose, double feathers. Plumage fades from almost black to grayish-brown, with whitish ruff at base of neck; skin of face and neck blue; legs dark grayish-brown; bill blackish; eyes yellow, grayish-brown or reddish.

DIET: Fruits, shoots, flowers, and seeds, plus small animals.

BREEDING: During southern winter, from April to November. Nest a platform or circle of leaves, grass, bark, or sticks on ground, or under bush or tree. 5–11 eggs, dark grayish-green, incubated by male alone for 56 days. Chicks leave

nest soon after hatching, but cared for by male for about 18 months. Female may stay nearby or leave to mate with another male.

LIFESTYLE: Almost as big as the ostrich, but with much smaller wings, the emu has a very similar

lifestyle in the open forests, scrub, and dry grasslands of its native Australia. It feeds selectively on high-quality food items, including insects and other small animals. Such foods are often scarce in the more arid regions, and flocks of emus wander vast distances across the continent in search of food.

Emus must also drink every day. This once prevented them from living on the drier grasslands, but the provision of water supplies for sheep and other livestock has enabled them to extend their range across much of the continent.

The breeding roles of emus are partly reversed, since the male does all the incubation while the larger female defends the nest with loud, booming calls. Many females abandon the incubating males and move away to mate again.

STORMCHASERS
Nomadic flocks of emus follow erratic rainstorms to feed on plants sprouting from the wet ground, using a highly-developed instinct for tracking rain clouds and other weather patterns.

BROWN KIWI

Apteryx australis
Family: APTERYGIDAE
Order: APTERYGIFORMES

NEW
ZEALAND

DISTRIBUTION: Native forests, pine plantations, and scrub of New Zealand, in scattered populations.

SIZE: Length 27.5in (70cm); weight 3.8–8.5lb (1.7–3.8kg); female larger than male.

APPEARANCE: Plump, flightless bird with thin feathers rather like hair, and no visible wings or tail. Long, flexible bill with nostrils near tip and large, sensitive whiskers around base. Plumage and legs brownish; bill yellowish to horn colored; eyes very small.

DIET: Insects and insect grubs, spiders, earthworms, and berries.

BREEDING: In late winter. Nest a hollow, unlined or lined with leaves and leaf mold, in a burrow, under tree roots or in a hollow log. 1–2 very large white eggs, incubated by male for 65–85 days. Chicks hatch well developed. Leave nest after 5 days, living on egg yolk. Cared for by male for some time.

LIFESTYLE: The skulking, nocturnal brown kiwi behaves less like a bird and more like a mammal. It sniffs and probes through the leaf litter and soil like a badger, looking for worms, grubs, and other prey. With its hair-like plumage, it even looks like a mammal. Such a bird could have evolved only in a land such as New Zealand, where there are no native ground-living mammals. This left the badger "niche" vacant for a suitably adapted bird. The kiwi is equipped for the job with a well developed sense of smell – something that is almost unique among birds. Its nostrils are at the end of its long, probing bill, so it can detect underground prey by scent as well as touch. Its eyes are small for a nocturnal bird, but since it lives in dense cover, in a world of scent and sound, it does not need to see well. If alarmed it runs away through the undergrowth on its powerful legs, protected from thorns by its thick, hairy plumage.

ELUSIVE ICON
Although famous as the emblem of New Zealand, the brown kiwi has such secretive habits that few New Zealanders have seen one, and some aspects of its life are still a mystery.

Kiwis live in pairs, defending their territories with shrieking calls. The female lays a huge egg that is a quarter of her own weight, with a very large yolk.

The brown kiwi has suffered badly from forest clearance over the past 200 years. It also makes easy prey for introduced predators such as cats and foxes, and is now common only in areas such as Stewart Island, where it has no enemies.

WESTERN CAPERCAILLIE

Tetrao urogallus
Family: TETRAONIDAE
Order: GALLIFORMES

DISTRIBUTION: Conifer woods and scrub of northern and central Europe, from Scotland and northwest Spain to the Balkans, and from Scandinavia east across Russia and Siberian taiga.

SIZE: Length 24–34in (60–87cm); weight 3.7–11.1lb (1.7–5.1kg); male much larger than female.

APPEARANCE: Turkeylike bird with feathered, brown to gray legs. Male dark gray with black throat and face, red eyebrow, and pale bill. Chestnut wings and shoulders, with white on flanks and glossy green breast mottled with white. Belly mottled blackish and white. Female brown to buff, mottled with white and black, with chestnut breast and dark gray bill.

DIET: Buds and shoots of conifer trees, seeds, grasses, berries, and fruits. Chicks eat insects.

BREEDING: In spring. Female makes scrape in undergrowth or at the foot of a tree, lined with plant material and debris. 5–8 pale yellowish-buff eggs, incubated by female alone for 24–29 days. Chicks can fly at 2–3 weeks.

LIFESTYLE: The capercaillie is the largest of the grouse. The male is huge compared to the more conservatively colored female, but both sexes spend a lot of time in the trees, roosting on branches at night and feeding on pine needles in winter. In the summer and fall they feed mainly on the ground, gathering the soft shoots and berries of woodland plants such as bilberry, cloudberry, and horsetails.

On early spring mornings the males gather on traditional display grounds (leks) to compete for the favors of the females, each trying to mate with as many females as possible. Fanning their turkeylike tails, drooping their wings, and puffing out their bristly throat feathers, they strut across the ground with slow, deliberate steps, stretching their heads up to produce their strange gurgling, popping song. The song is often answered by nearby males, and rivals often square up to each other with their neck feathers inflated. Such confrontations often lead to fights, and some males may be injured so badly that they die. The males are also aggressive toward people, dogs, and even cars.

BUBBLING CALL
The male capercaillie's courtship call is a bizarre crescendo of bubbling and gurgling notes, climaxing with a loud pop like a cork being released from a champagne bottle.

SAGE GROUSE

Centrocercus urophasianus
Family: TETRAONIDAE
Order: GALLIFORMES

DISTRIBUTION: Sagebrush plains, hills and deserts of North America, from Washington state and Saskatchewan to eastern California and western Colorado.

SIZE: Length, males 26–30in (66–76cm); weight, males 5–7lb (2.3–3.2kg). Females are slightly shorter and less weighty.

APPEARANCE: Sturdy, plump, and chickenlike with long, pointed tail. Female barred and mottled yellowish-brown, with black belly; legs feathered, grayish; bill dark; eyes dark brown. Male much bigger, with blackish throat and bib separated by white collar from dark "V" pattern on neck; large ruff of white feathers on breast with erectable black hairlike feathers and two inflatable air sacs of yellow skin; comb of yellow skin over each eye.

DIET: Leaves of sagebrush, and of other plants in summer.

BREEDING: In spring. Males promiscuous. Nest a scrape on the ground, made by female, lined with plant material and debris, often under sagebrush. 6–9 pale olive to buffish-olive eggs, incubated by female alone for 25–27 days. Young hatch well-developed and leave nest almost immediately; cared for by female, and fledge in 7–10 days. Chicks eat mainly insects.

OPPOSITES ATTRACT
The female sage grouse's mottled plumage (*left*) camouflages her from predators when nesting. The ruffed male is in spectacular contrast.

LIFESTYLE: Largest of American grouse at the size of a pheasant, the sage grouse is closely tied to the sagebrush plant community. As well as serving as the species' staple fall and winter food, the aromatic sagebrush shrubs provide cover year-round among which the grouse can hide from predators, such as coyotes, ground squirrels, badgers, and ravens.

The males, twice the bulk of the females, display communally to prospective mates at a traditional site, called a lek (Swedish for "play"). Up to 400 males may display at a single lek. Their ritualized displays begin with each male strutting about and inflating his neck sacs until they almost touch the ground. With his tail fanned and held erect, he suddenly throws back his head, lowers his stiffly held wings almost to the ground, and deflates the air sacs to produce a loud popping sound.

Sage grouse have declined due to habitat destruction and fragmentation and human disturbance. Most threatened are those isolated in the Gunnison Basin area of south-west Colorado, though now recognized as a separate species. They are only half the usual size of the sage grouse.

COMMON PHEASANT

Phasianus colchicus
Family: PHASIANIDAE
Order: GALLIFORMES

DISTRIBUTION: Originally only in woodlands, marshes, and cultivated areas of central and eastern Asia; introduced to Europe, North America, Tasmania, New Zealand. In many countries where they have been introduced, common pheasants are artificially bred by the thousand and released for hunting. Many go wild.

NOISY ESCAPE
A startled pheasant gives an explosive crow of alarm and bursts into the air with a noisy whir of its rounded wings.

SIZE: Length 20.5–35.5in (52–90cm); weight 2.1–2.9lb (0.95–1.32kg); male considerably larger than female.

APPEARANCE: Male ranges from bright reddish-brown to dark purplish-brown, with rufous lower back and rump, and long, pointed, copper-brown tail; head and neck iridescent dark green, often with white collar; small ear tufts; large patch of red skin around eye. Female mottled rufous and blackish, with shorter tail. Interbreeding between various species introduced at different times has created several plumage variations.

DIET: Seeds, nuts, acorns, berries, leaves, fruits, and insects.

BREEDING: Nests in spring or early summer. Female makes shallow scrape, unlined or thinly lined with plant material. 7–15 olive, olive-brown, brown, or bluish-gray eggs, incubated by female alone for 23–27 days. Chicks can fly at about 12 days old, and are independent at 10–12 weeks.

LIFESTYLE: A great opportunist, the pheasant is ready to take advantage of any available food source, and this has allowed it to flourish in woodlands and farmland where it has been introduced as a gamebird. In its native Asia it is a bird of open forests with grassland in upland valleys; here it forages for a wide variety of seeds, fruits, and small animals. Males are fiercely territorial and rivals crow loudly, face up to each other with lowered heads and ruffled neck plumage, then leap into the attack like fighting cocks, striking with the sharp spurs on the backs of their feet. The victor displays his vivid plumage to any females in the vicinity, running around them with his wings trailing and red facial wattles inflated.

WILD TURKEY

Meleagris gallopavo
Family: MELEAGRIDIDAE
Order: GALLIFORMES

DISTRIBUTION: In open woodlands, grassy clearings and scrublands, scattered across North America, from southern Canada south through the United States to Florida and central Mexico.

SIZE: Length 33–47in (85–120cm); weight 4–10kg (8.8–2lb).

APPEARANCE: Slightly smaller and slimmer than domestic turkey. Male iridescent dark bronze-brown, with black-edged feathers; primaries barred with white; black tuft of feathers on breast; skin of head blue and pink, with red skin wattles; legs pale brown, with spurs; bill dark yellowish-brown; eyes dark. Female duller, often without breast tuft.

DIET: Seeds (including grains), nuts, fruits, leaves, tubers; insects and other invertebrates.

BREEDING: In spring, the males are promiscuous. The female makes a shallow scrape, thinly lined with plant material. Each female usually lays 10–13 pale buff or cream eggs, speckled and spotted with brown; sometimes, two females lay up to 26 in the same nest. Incubation by female for 28 days. Chicks cared for by female. Fledge at 6–10 days.

LIFESTYLE: The ancestor of the domestic turkey, this is North America's largest gamebird. Males are much bigger than females, standing about 8in (20cm) taller and weighing twice as much.

The wild turkey needs a mix of trees and grasses. The trees provide the birds with some of its food, cover in which to escape predators during the day, and roost-sites at night. The turkeys need the grassland for most of their food, both plant and animal.

Turkey chicks are rarely fed by their parents. Straight after hatching, they learn how to catch insects. These form almost their entire diet, and when the chicks are only a week old they may snap up as many as 4,000 grasshoppers and other insects each day. From about six weeks old, they gradually switch to eating more and more plant matter. Adults are omnivores, taking advantage of any suitable plant or animal food they find as they wander about, scratching in the soil or fallen leaves with their strong claws.

Before European settlers and their guns reached America, wild turkeys probably numbered tens of millions. Overhunting and habitat destruction resulted in huge declines and a great contraction of their range. Reintroduction of wild birds resulted in restocking of the species over much of its former range and also in new areas. Today, where they are not hunted or otherwise harassed, wild turkeys are happy to live close to humans, even in suburban gardens.

STRANGE LOVE SONG
The male turkey utters his well-known "gobbling" call during the breeding season to attract females to mate with him. The sound is audible to humans up to 1.5 miles (2.5km) away.

HELMETED GUINEAFOWL

Numida meleagris
Family: MELEAGRIDAE
Order: GALLIFORMES

DISTRIBUTION: Wide range of dry habitats, from forest edge to thorn thickets, scrub and semi-desert, most common in moist, well-wooded savanna grassland, especially where land is cultivated for maize or wheat; in much of Africa south of the Sahara, and in southwest Morocco; introduced to southwestern Arabia and Madagascar; domesticated form widespread worldwide.

SIZE: Length 21–23in (53–58cm); weight 2.25-3.75lb (1-1.5kg).

APPEARANCE: Medium-sized gamebird with a very small head, bearing a large, bony, brownish casque (the "helmet"), and a bulky, squarish body. Plumage blackish-gray, with rows of white spots and streaks; head and most of neck bare, blue or white; hairlike feathers on hind neck black; cere (fleshy pad at base of mainly brownish bill) and hanging skin wattles red and blue; tuft of white bristles over nostrils in two races.

DIET: Seeds (including grains), bulbs, roots and other plant food; also grasshoppers, termites, and other insects, earthworms, mollusks, and other invertebrates.

BREEDING: Nest is a scrape on ground, lined with grass and feathers, in long grass among dense cover; sometimes shared by 2 females. 6–12 (rarely up to 20), cream or buff eggs, speckled with brown and white. Incubated by female for 24–28 days. Chicks fledge in 4 weeks.

LIFESTYLE: Largest and most widespread and abundant of the six species of guineafowls, the helmeted guineafowl lives in pairs in the breeding season, otherwise in flocks. Beginning with the Egyptians, over 4,000 years ago, various different peoples independently domesticated this adaptable guineafowl as a source of food.

BOLD DEFENDER
The helmeted
guineafowl is capable
of defending itself
against some predators
by buffeting them with
outstretched wings,
pecking with its
powerful bill, and
kicking out with its
strong feet.

BLUE PEAFOWL

Pavo cristatus
Family: PHASIANIDAE
Order: GALLIFORMES

DISTRIBUTION: Forests, scrub, and farmland in the Himalayas, India, Pakistan, and Sri Lanka; introduced to parks and gardens worldwide.

SIZE: Length of male 79–90in (200–229cm), female 34in (86cm); male weight 9–13lb (4–6kg), female 6–9lb (2.7–4kg).

APPEARANCE: Large pheasant with crest of tufted quills; male has blue head, neck, and breast, with white cheeks and stripe above eye; metallic green back with very long train of elongated tail coverts dotted with iridescent eyespots; female has bronze-green neck and breast; white face and belly; brown back with no train. Whitish bill and legs.

DIET: Seeds, shoots, berries, insects, and other small animals.

BREEDING: Polygamous male guards a harem of females. Each female nests in a scrape on the ground, laying 4–6 creamy-white eggs; incubation 28 days, by female alone; chicks leave nest soon after hatching.

LIFESTYLE: Familiar as a half-tame ornamental bird all over the world, the spectacular blue peafowl is a native of hilly forests in the Himalayas and Indian subcontinent. There it feeds in thick cover by day, and roosts in trees for the night. It also forages over farmland, gathering a wide variety of seeds, fruits, and other plant material, as well as insects, lizards, and small mammals such as mice. It has regular habits, often roosting in the same tree each night and returning to the same feeding site. It is very wary – as it needs to be, since the long train of the male impedes its movements and makes it very vulnerable to predators such as big cats. If it senses danger it sounds the alarm with a loud call as it makes its escape, and acts as a sentinel for other forest animals.

For most of the year blue peafowl live in small groups or family parties, but during the breeding season the male becomes solitary and territorial. He claims an open patch in the forest as a display ground – returning to it every season – and defends it against neighboring males by displaying, calling, and even fighting with his sharp claws and spurs. These battles can last a whole day.

When a female comes near, the male turns away from her and erects his train into an immense, rustling fan, dotted with iridescent eyespots. He backs towards her, and as she steps aside he suddenly swivels round to dazzle her with the full glory of his display. He arches the fan forward so it almost engulfs the female, shivering the plumes to make them rustle loudly. If the female is sufficiently impressed she may then join his harem and allow him to mate with her.

IRIDESCENT TRAIN
The long "tail" of the male peafowl – or peacock – is actually composed of extra-long upper tail coverts that sprout from the bird's back, hiding its true tail feathers.

RED JUNGLE FOWL

Gallus gallus
Family: PHASIANIDAE
Order: GALLIFORMES

DISTRIBUTION: Inhabits a wide range of wooded habitats, from thorn forests to coastal mangroves; mainly in jungle and scrubland with dense undergrowth and clearings or cultivated land for feeding. Native range from north-east India east to China and south to Sumatra, Java and Bali.

SIZE: Length, males 25.5–29.5in (65–75cm), females 16.5-18in (42–46cm); weight, males 1.5–3.2lb (0.67–1.45kg) females 1.1–2.3lb (0.49–1.05kg).

APPEARANCE: Male has long, glossy red neck plumes (hackles) and tail coverts and long dark greenish wing coverts and tail feathers and leg spurs; female has streaked red-brown, yellowish and blackish plumage; lacks ornamental feathers and leg spurs; has small area of bare skin on head.

DIET: Seeds, fruits, shoots, other plant matter; insects and spiders, snails and other invertebrates.

BREEDING: Season varies; often during dry season in spring. Nest a simple scrape in ground, lined with grass and other vegetation, and hidden in dense cover. 4–9 pale buff to reddish-brown eggs, incubated by female for 18–20 days. She cares for young, which fledge in about 10–14 days.

LIFESTYLE: This is the ancestor of the domestic chicken. Today, there are over twice as many chickens in the world as humans. Wild jungle fowls are very shy, and more often heard than seen. Males mate with several females: the flock have a distinct peck order, like chickens.

OSTENTATIOUS
The male crows like the domesticated rooster to proclaim his territory and attract a harem of females. His red comb and wattles and long erectile neck feathers are there to impress.

KORI BUSTARD

Ardeotis kori
Family: OTIDIDAE
Order: GRUIFORMES

DISTRIBUTION: Variety of flat, arid, mainly open habitats, such as thorn bush, savanna, and grasslands; two separate populations, one in east Africa and one in southern Africa.

SIZE: Length 35–47in (90–120cm); weight 13–42lb (5.9–19kg).

APPEARANCE: Very large ground-dwelling bird with daggerlike bill and straggly black and gray crest on crown. Upperparts brown with fine black markings; upper wing coverts white with black spots, showing as bar when wings closed; tail black-and-white; underparts white, with black at base of neck and on shoulders; chin, throat, and neck finely barred gray and legs dull yellowish to grayish; eyes orange-brown to yellow; bill gray, yellowish or horn-colored.

DIET: Chiefly insects, especially locusts, grasshoppers, also other invertebrates, small vertebrates and vegetable matter, including seeds, bulbs and wild melons.

BREEDING: Season variable, related to rains. Males may mate with several females. 2 pale olive eggs, streaked with grayish and dark brown, laid on ground (no nest) and incubated by female for about 25 days. Young fed by female at first. Fledge at about 5 weeks.

LIFESTYLE: This imposing bird may live in flocks outside the breeding season. Males are considerably bigger and much heavier than females. Indeed, the male is one of the heaviest of all the world's flying birds.

At the start of the breeding season, the male puts on a spectacular courtship display. He swells his throat, fluffing out his feathers to reveal their white undersides so that he appears white almost all over, rather like a huge living powder puff. At the same time, he raises his fanned tail over his back and droops his wings, uttering drumlike booming sounds.

Kori bustards forage by striding slowly and sedately, on the lookout for a wide range of food, from swarms of locusts, other insects, lizards, snakes, rodents, eggs and nestling birds to seeds and other plant material. The bustards often turn up at bush fires, snapping up small animals fleeing from the flames, and also eating the bodies of small animals that fail to escape. Over much of its range the kori bustard is threatened by hunting, habitat destruction, disturbance, and colliding in flight with electricity cables, fences, and vehicles.

HITCHING A RIDE
Carmine bee-eaters often rides on a kori bustard's broad back, flying down to snap up some of the insects disturbed by the great bird as its walks.

GREATER ROADRUNNER

Geococcyx californianus
Family: CUCULIDAE
Order: CUCULIFORMES

DISTRIBUTION: Most abundant in scrubby desert and mesquite groves; less common in chaparral, and dry, open, pine-oak woodlands; in the southwestern United States and central Mexico.

SIZE: Length 20–24in (51–61cm); weight 7.8–12oz (220–340g); males slightly larger than females.

APPEARANCE: Magpie-sized bird with longish, heavy, hooked bill and prominent, spiky crest on head; longish, sturdy legs; short, rounded wings; long, graduated tail. Upperparts dark brownish with bronze sheen, with pale buff-edges to feathers giving mottled appearance; buff-spotted, blackish crest; wings have a white crescent on the primary flight feathers; tail tipped with white; underparts and neck whitish with dark brown streaks; legs gray; bill blackish; eyes brown, ringed with yellow; patch of bare skin behind eye, white and orange in male, blue and orange in female.

DIET: Mainly lizards and snakes, also very wide range of other prey, from insects and scorpions to small rodents and small birds, including nestlings and hummingbirds; carcasses of animals killed on roads; also some fruit, especially of cacti, and seeds.

BREEDING: Late February-October, depending on location. Makes neat, shallow, saucer-shaped nest of twigs, lined with grass, leaves, roots, feathers and debris, in bush, cactus or low tree. 2–6 white eggs with a chalky cream covering, incubated mainly by male, especially at night, for 17–18 days. Chicks hatch helpless; cared for by both parents. Fledge at 17–19 days. Sometimes rears two broods.

LIFESTYLE: As its name suggests, the greater roadrunner is the larger of two unusual species of ground-dwelling cuckoos (the other being the lesser roadrunner of Mexico

PROCESSING PREY
The fast, agile greater roadrunner can outrun many lizards. Striking its capture on a hard surface not only kills it but breaks up the skeleton so it is easier to swallow.

and Central America). Made famous by the cartoon character, the real roadrunner can run at speeds of up to 18mph (24kmh) when fleeing danger or pursuing prey. It is one of the few animals that attacks rattlesnakes. A pair sometimes hunts together, circling it and alternating onslaughts. To kill this dangerous reptile, the roadrunner grabs the snake just behind its head, then batters it against the ground or stones. Roadrunners live in pairs, defending their territory all year. The male displays to the female by wings and tail drooping. Courtship includes chases, as well as displays in which the male raises his wings, erects or wags his tail and bows, while proffering a mouse or other prey. He also calls to his mate from a perch with a mournful dove-like cooing, descending in pitch.

DUSKY BROADBILL

Corydon sumatranus
Family: EURYLAIMIDAE
Order: PASSERIFORMES

DISTRIBUTION: High in the canopy of the forests of southeast Asia, Sumatra and northwest Borneo, especially along streams.

SIZE: Length 9.5–11in (24–27.5cm); weight about 5oz (140g).

APPEARANCE: Stout-bodied bird with large head, massive, very broad, flattened, hooked bill and short tail; third and fourth toes partly fused. Color dull blackish, with buffish throat and narrow white band near tip of tail; concealed yellowish-orange streak on back; wingbar broad, white; legs blackish; bill pinkish or yellowish. Juveniles are browner, with a darker throat, and lack orange patch on back.

DIET: Mostly insects; also spiders, snails and other invertebrates; reported to eat vertebrate prey such as small lizards. Their large, strongly hooked bills suggest that they may specialize in eating relatively big prey, up to 4 inches

(10cm) long. They usually snatch their prey from the foliage after a brief flight, but sometimes leap into the air from a perch to snap up a large flying insect. Very occasionally, they may supplement their diet with fruit.

BREEDING: Mainly in wet season; several birds may help to build a pear-shaped nest of stems, roots, grass, leaves, spider webs, and other material, with an opening at the side, hung by a cord of plant fibers from a branch, usually over a river. 2–4 speckled eggs, incubated by both parents. Incubation and fledging periods unknown.

LIFESTYLE: Dusky broadbills are highly social birds, living in groups of up to 10 birds, even when breeding. Birds in its range start nesting from the end of the dry season, so that their young hatch in the wet season, when there is plenty of suitable prey available to

feed them. Farther south, they begin earlier, during the wettest part of the year, and the breeding season can last up to 10 months. The remarkable hanging nest is often 6.5 feet (2m) or more tall. The sticky spider webs the birds add to the outside and bottom of the nest are used by the birds for attaching a wide range of material, such as caterpillar droppings, insect cocoons, spiders' egg-bags and living green leaves. This provides superb camouflage, helping to prevent any predators (such as snakes, lizards, or rats) agile enough to reach their delicately suspended nests from raiding their contents. Dusky broadbills are most active at dawn and dusk. Groups are often located by their screaming notes, piercing whistles, croaks, and rattling laughs.

WELL NAMED
Broadbills are named for their very wide bills. The remarkably large, distinctly hooked bill is probably the widest of any perching bird.

BLUE-WINGED PITTA

> *Pitta moluccensis*
> Family: PITTIDAE
> Order: PASSERIFORMES

DISTRIBUTION: Breeds in southern China, Indo-China, Malaysian peninsula and perhaps Borneo, in various habitats, from open woodland and bamboo thickets to dense rain forest; northern birds migrate to winter in Malaysian peninsula, Sumatra and Borneo.

SIZE: Length 7–8in (18–20.5cm); weight 1.8–3oz (50–87g).

APPEARANCE: Small, with plump breast, strong bill, longish legs, and short tail. Upperparts greenish, with bright violet-blue wing coverts and blackish outer wings, with big white wing-patches in flight; rump violet- blue; tail black with narrow blue band at tip; head black, with paler buff-chestnut band above eye; throat white; underparts buff, shading to crimson on belly and flanks; legs pinkish, feet and toes yellowish; bill black; eyes dark brown. Juveniles much duller.

DIET: Mainly insects and spiders; also other invertebrates.

BREEDING: Season variable. Builds large, untidy spherical nest on the ground of twigs, roots, grasses, leaves and mosses, with side entrance, often between tree roots near water. 4–6 white or cream eggs, heavily marked with purple; incubated by both parents, probably for 15–17 days. Chicks probably fledge at 14–21 days.

LIFESTYLE: Like other pittas, the blue-winged species looks rather like a plump, long-legged thrush. Its stocky body, sturdy bill, large eyes, strong legs, and short tail are adaptations for a life spent largely on the forest floor. Pittas are renowned for the jewel-like beauty of the adult plumage, and this species is no exception. However, the brilliant colors are restricted chiefly to the bird's underside. This makes it surprisingly hard to spot in the gloom of the forest understory. In addition, it is a shy, secretive bird that generally reacts to danger by standing motionless, its back turned towards an intruder, making it even harder to see. If pressed, though, the pitta makes it escape with rapid, bounding hops or by flying for a short distance just above the ground to hide in dense cover. Often, the only clue to its presence is the loud, whistling calls, which it utters mainly in the breeding season, when pairs defend their territories against rivals. Blue-winged pittas migrate at night, when they may form loose flocks. On migration and in winter, they occur not only in wooded country, but also visit other habitats, such as mangroves and scrubland. In places, they are caught for food and for cage birds.

LEAFING THROUGH
The blue-winged pitta forages by flicking fallen leaves aside with its bill to expose prey ranging from ants or snails to large crickets. It also probes in soil for earthworms.

SUPERB LYREBIRD

Menura novaehollandiae
Family: MENURIDAE
Order: PASSERIFORMES

DISTRIBUTION: Dense forests and woodland, to above snowline, in southeastern Australia. Introduced to Tasmania.

SIZE: Length 29–33in (74–84cm); weight 2–2.5lb (950–1150g); male larger than female.

APPEARANCE: Large pheasantlike bird with slightly crested crown. Rich brown above, grayish-brown below; throat tinged rufous. Bare, bluish-black facial skin; brown eyes with pale eye-ring; gray legs and bill. Male has very long tail, with two broad lyre-shaped feathers, two slender ribbonlike feathers, and 12 lacy filamentous feathers.

DIET: Insects, grubs, and worms.

BREEDING: June to October. Male is polygamous. Builds large domed nest of sticks, leaves, roots, bark and moss, with side entrance, lined with feathers, on ground under cover. Single gray or purplish-brown egg, streaked and spotted,

incubated by female for up to 50 days. Chick fledges at about 47 days, but is fed by female for up to eight months.

LIFESTYLE: Like many birds with extravagant plumage, such as the birds of paradise, the superb lyrebird is an elusive inhabitant of dense forests. Its strongholds are the temperate and subtropical rainforests of southeastern Australia. At night it roosts high in the forest canopy, beyond the reach of ground predators, although it does not fly well, preferring to glide. By day it forages for food on the forest floor, digging in the leaf litter and soil and ripping away the loose bark of fallen trees to get at small animals such as worms, beetle grubs, spiders, and centipedes.

In late winter the male claims a patch of forest as his own territory, heaps up a series of mounds to use as stages, and starts to sing and display by spreading his tail plumes in a glorious silvery fan and arching them forward over his head. When he attracts a female he dances around her, quivering his tail and making clicking and ringing calls. Once they have mated, the female goes off to nest on her own.

During the nineteenth century superb lyrebirds were hunted for their plumes, which were used to decorate hats. They were saved by the early bird protection societies, but now they are coming under pressure again as their forest habitat is gradually destroyed.

EXPERT MIMIC
Male lyrebirds are superb mimics, able to copy the calls of at least 16 other birds. They even copy artificial sounds, such as car alarms and ringing telephones.

BARN SWALLOW

Hirundo rustica
Family: HIRUNDINIDAE
Order: PASSERIFORMES

DISTRIBUTION: Breeds throughout Europe, Asia, and North America, excluding far north, in open country near water. Winters in southern hemisphere.

SIZE: Length 7in (18cm); weight 0.4–0.9oz (11–25g).

APPEARANCE: Slim, elegant bird with long, tapering wings and deeply-forked tail. Short black bill with wide gape. Dark metallic blue upperparts; chestnut forehead; dark chestnut chin and throat separated from creamy to rufous-buff underparts by dark blue band.

DIET: Airborne insects, particularly large flies.

BREEDING: Breeds from May to September. Pair builds cup-shaped nest of mud and straw, lined with feathers, on ledge or under cover in cave or open shed. 4–5 white eggs, spotted with red, incubated mainly by female for 14–15 days. Young fledge at about 21 days.

LIFESTYLE: Fast and wonderfully agile in the air, with gleaming plumage and long tail streamers, the barn swallow is one of the most elegant of all insect-hunting birds. It catches all its prey in flight, but unlike the superficially similar swift it often perches on high vantage points and darts out to intercept its victims. It frequently hunts at low level over pastures and stockyards, swooping around the feet of grazing cattle and sheep to snap up the insects they disturb. It does them a favor by eating a lot of bloodsucking horseflies, gadflies, and parasitic blowflies. It drinks on the wing, skimming across pools to scoop up mouthfuls of water.

Like most other insect-eaters it migrates to the tropics during the northern winter, flying up to 6,800 miles (11,000km) to reach the grasslands of South America and southern Africa. In spring it returns north to breed, penetrating as far as the southern fringes of the Arctic tundra.

Barn swallows often live up to their name by nesting in farm buildings, particularly cattle sheds which offer shelter, warmth, and a steady supply of flies. But they are bold birds, quite prepared to raise families in places used regularly by people; they often nest in porches, carports, and backyard sheds, flying in and out through gaping doors and broken windows.

At the end of the breeding season barn swallows perch on overhead wires in noisy groups, and gather in mass roosts in reedbeds with other swallows and martins. These gatherings are the prelude to the southward migration, which may last for two months or more.

Like all insect-eating farmland birds, the barn swallow has been badly hit by the widespread use of insecticides, which destroy its food supply. Yet it is still common wherever it can find places to nest and rear its young.

FORKED TAIL
The barn swallow's long tail streamers give it breathtaking agility in the air. The streamers of an adult male are longer than those of a female, and a juvenile has the shortest of all.

BANK SWALLOW

Riparia riparia
Family: HIRUNDINIDAE
Order: PASSERIFORMES

DISTRIBUTION: Breeds in open country, usually near water, in North America, Europe and Asia, north to the tundra zone. Winters in South America, Africa south of Sahara, northern India, and Southeast Asia.

SIZE: Length 5–5.5in (12–14cm); weight 0.5oz (13–14g)

APPEARANCE: Small swallow with short bill and relatively short, only slightly forked tail; sandy brown above, off-white below with brown breast band.

DIET: Small flying insects such as mosquitoes, caught on the wing; also airborne spiders.

BREEDING: Breeds in early spring, in colonies. Digs nesting tunnel in steep, soft, often sandy bank or cliff, lining nesting chamber with soft grass, leaves, and feathers. 4–6 white eggs, incubated by both sexes for 14–15 days; chicks fledge in 19 days. Usually 2 broods.

LIFESTYLE: The delicate-looking bank swallow is the smallest and weakest of the swallows and martins. It has a fluttering, jerky flight, without the elegance of the closely related barn swallow. But its agility on the wing makes it a very effective aerial hunter, able to twist and turn to follow flies and snap them up in its small, but wide-gaping bill. It feeds almost exclusively on tiny airborne insects such as mosquitoes and midges, often hunting low over the surface of lakes, rivers, marshes, and flooded sand and gravel pits.

These flooded pits make ideal breeding sites, with plenty of prey and steep, often sandy banks where the birds can dig their nesting burrows. Each pair shares the bank with many others, forming a breeding colony that may number many hundreds of pairs. There are usually many more holes than breeding pairs, however, because although the bank swallows return to the same site each spring, they often discover that the old tunnels are infested with fleas and other parasites, and abandon them.

In late summer the bank swallows leave the nesting colony and gather in mass roosts for the night, usually in dense reedbeds. With barn swallows, they may form huge mixed roosts of up to 250,000 birds. Eventually the roosts break up as the birds fly off on migration.

BUSY COLONY
In spring the Bank swallow colony becomes a scene of frenzied activity as the mated pairs clear out old burrows or dig new ones, ready for the first brood of the season.

YELLOW WAGTAIL

Motacilla flava
Family: MOTACILLIDAE
Order: PASSERIFORMES

DISTRIBUTION: Breeds on damp grasslands, marshes, and boggy moors across most of Europe and Asia to coastal Alaska. Winters in tropical Asia and Africa.

SIZE: Length 6.5in (17cm); weight 0.4–0.9oz (11–26g).

APPEARANCE: Slender bird with long tail and long toes. Male has greenish shoulders and wings, two pale wing-bars; blackish-brown tail with white edges. Crown bright yellow, black, white, or bluish-gray in breeding season depending on local race. Black legs. Female similar but duller.

DIET: Mainly insects, plus spiders and other small invertebrates.

BREEDING: In spring and summer. Builds well concealed cup-shaped nest of grasses, stems, and roots, lined with hair, on ground. 5–6 pale buff or gray eggs, speckled with yellowish-buff or brownish-buff, incubated mainly by female for 12–14 days. Young cared for by both parents. Leave nest at 10–13 days; fledge at about 17 days.

LIFESTYLE: The graceful yellow wagtail is a summer visitor in the north, where it is associated with wet meadows and watersides. Many spend the winter in drier habitats such as the African plains; there they feed in busy flocks at the feet of grazing animals such as zebras and antelopes, running to snap up insects disturbed by their hooves, and fluttering up to snatch flies. They may even pick ticks and other bloodsuckers from the animals' skins. On their return north in spring they keep up the habit, following cattle and horses instead. In winter, and while on migration, they gather in hundreds to spend the night in mass roosts.

In their winter habitats all yellow wagtails look much the same, but before migrating north the males acquire breeding plumage that varies according to their breeding range. There are some 18 races; some are so distinctive that they have different common names, like the black-headed wagtail of southeast Europe.

On arrival in the north, yellow wagtails pair up and claim breeding territories. The males sing from perches or in display-flights, rising steeply and parachuting down with their tails spread and legs dangling. Yet the territories often overlap, and the birds feed in company throughout the summer.

LOCAL COLOR
The "black-headed wagtail" is the most distinctive of many local races. In other races breeding males may have greenish, gray, or blue-gray heads, but females are all very alike.

SKY LARK

Alauda arvensis
Family: ALAUDIDAE
Order: PASSERIFORMES

DISTRIBUTION: Breeds on farmland and open country from Europe and northernmost North Africa across Asia, except in the far north, to northeastern Siberia and China. Northern and eastern populations move south for the winter. Introduced to Australia, New Zealand, Japan, and Vancouver Island, Canada.

SIZE: Length 7in (18cm); weight 1–1.8oz (29–51g).

APPEARANCE: Small brownish bird with triangular wings, small crest, long hind claws, and longish tail. Upperparts brown, with darker streaks; wings darker, with white trailing edges; tail edged white; underparts buffish-white. Legs and bill yellowish-brown; eyes brown.

DIET: Mainly seeds and leaves, plus insects, spiders, and other invertebrates.

BREEDING: From late spring. The nest is a shallow cup made of dry grasses on the ground, often in a tussock, and lined with finer grasses. 3–4 greenish-gray or creamy-gray eggs, heavily mottled with dark grayish-brown, incubated by female for about 11 days. Young are cared for by both parents; they leave the nest at 9–10 days and fledge at about 20 days.

LIFESTYLE: Celebrated for its glorious aerial song, the sky lark is a bird of open, grassy landscapes from high hills to low-lying coastal saltmarshes and dunes. It spends much of its time feeding on the ground, walking or shuffling along with its body held low, picking up seeds and occasional insects from the soil or from low-growing plants. It sometimes digs for recently-sown arable seeds, and may uproot the seedlings of wheat and other cereals to eat the sprouting grain. When alarmed, it crouches close to the ground, then suddenly flies up to make its escape.

The male may perform its song flight throughout the year, except during its late summer molt. The bird climbs vertically into the air to a great height, then hangs on fluttering wings for several minutes while pouring out a liquid, silvery stream of warbling song. It then spirals or parachutes down to the ground –often still singing – and then falls silent while another sky lark rises to take its place.

STEEP DECLINE
Modern agricultural methods have led to a steep decline in sky lark numbers in northern and western Europe, but its glorious song is still a common feature of open country.

BLUE-BACKED FAIRY-BLUEBIRD

Irena puella
Family: IRENIDAE
Order: PASSERIFORMES

DISTRIBUTION: Scattered populations in dense forests of southeast Asia, from southern India (probably) and Nepal to the island of Palawan, in the Philippines.

SIZE: Length 10.5in (27cm); weight 1.8–2.5oz (51–70.3g).

APPEARANCE: Thrush-sized bird with dense, fluffy plumage. Male's upperparts intense iridescent blue, with velvety-black cheeks, chin, wings, tail and underparts; upper- and under-tail coverts blue; legs and bill blackish; eyes red. Female dull bluish-green; primary wing feathers and tail dark brown; black patch around eye.

DIET: Mainly fruit, especially figs, and including berries; also nectar from various flowers and some insects.

BREEDING: Season varies; in India mainly February to April. Nest, built by female, is a flimsy platform of twigs, covered by a layer of rootlets, leaf ribs and mosses, with a central cup lined with moss; sited from about 16 feet (5m) high up in a fork of a tree amid dense foliage. Eggs usually 2, occasionally 3, greenish white, olive-grey, buff or reddish grey, with brown, grey and purple streaks and blotches; incubated by female alone.

LIFESTYLE: Together with its close relative, the black-mantled (or Philippine) fairy-bluebird, which replaces it in most of the Philippine islands, the blue-backed (or Asian) fairy-bluebird is classified in a family of its own. The fairy-bluebirds are one of only two bird families that are found only in the Oriental faunal region.

These beautiful birds are usually restricted to undisturbed, moist, semi-deciduous or evergreen forests, though they may occur in other habitats, such as coffee plantations. Pairs or small, loose flocks roam through the forest,

ELECTRIC BLUE
The male is seen at his best when he perches in a shaft of sunlight in a clearing, his iridescent body plumage catching the rays to create a vision of brilliant metallic blue.

searching for fruit-bearing trees, often in the company of hornbills, green pigeons, and other fruit-eating birds. They feed mainly high up, at canopy level, and may gather briefly in larger numbers in places where many trees come into fruit at the same time. The birds maintain contact with one another as they move about among the dense forest foliage with loud, liquid, whistling cries, and in flight with sharp, repeated calls.

PALMCHAT

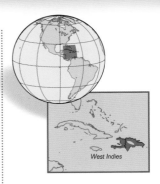
West Indies

Dulus dominicus
Family: DULIDAE
Order: PASSERIFORMES

DISTRIBUTION: In open woodland, among palm trees and plantations, and in clumps of pine trees, at altitudes of up to about 4,500 feet (1,370m) on the island of Hispaniola (divided between the countries of Dominica and Haiti) and the offshore Haitiian island of Gonave in the West Indies.

SIZE: Length 7in (18cm); weight about 1.5oz (42g).

APPEARANCE: Small bird with stout, pointed bill, short wings and long tail. Color of upperparts grayish-white to olive-brown, with darker head; wings yellowish-green; rump dark green; underparts yellowish-white, striped with dark brown; legs blackish; bill brownish; eyes brown. Juvenile has dark brown throat and a buff rump.

DIET: Berries and flowers.

BREEDING: March to June. Breeds communally, as many as 30 pairs making a large communal nest up to 3.3 feet (1m) across, made of twigs, usually woven around trunk and bases of the fronds high in a royal palm tree. Some nest in pines, with only a few pairs making smaller nests. Pairs have separate nest entrances and nest chambers, thinly lined with fine grass and shredded bark. Usually 4 white eggs, heavily spotted with dark purplish gray.

LIFESTYLE: The palmchat is the only member of its family, found on just two Caribbean islands. Ornithologists sometimes classify this unique species within the same family as the waxwings of Eurasia and North America and the North American silky flycatchers, though it lacks their soft, dense, silk-like plumage and its bill is heavier.

VARIED POSTURE
When searching for food, palmchats have an alert air as they move through trees and bushes. This contrasts with their resting posture, upright with the tail pointing down.

Palmchats spend almost all their time up in the trees. The birds rest and roost in the nests all year. They often perch so close to one another that their bodies touch. However, they also exhibit bouts of aggressiveness toward rivals, which are usually accompanied by the whole group suddenly erupting in loud, raucous calls.

Palmchats are generally very noisy and are among the most conspicuous birds on the islands of Hispaniola. They are widespread and locally abundant in most parts of the islands, but are not found in rain forests or at higher altitudes.

The communal nests, which can be as large as a stork's nest, are huge, including very large sticks for the size of the birds. Doubtless, these impressive structures give adults, eggs, and young effective protection from predators.

NORTH AMERICAN DIPPER

Cinclus mexicanus
Family: CINCLIDAE
Order: PASSERIFORMES

DISTRIBUTION: Along rocky streams down the western mountain chain of North America, northern Central America, from Alaska to Guatemala.

SIZE: Length 7–8in (18–20cm); weight 1.5–2.3oz (43–65g).

APPEARANCE: Thrush-sized, plump bird that has a very short tail, often cocked, and strong legs, giving appearance of an overgrown wren. Plumage sooty grey, with short white-feathers on the eyelids, particularly noticeable on the lower eyelids; legs yellowish; bill blackish; eyes dark brown. Juvenile has paler, mottled underparts and a pale bill.

DIET: Aquatic insects and their larvae, mainly caddisfly and mayfly larvae; also other invertebrates, such as worms and snails, as well as small fish and fish eggs.

BREEDING: May to June. Pair build large domed nest of moss, lined

with dead leaves, located in a steep bank or under a bridge over fast-flowing water, or under a waterfall, through which they fly to reach it; nest may be used for years or new one built on top of old one. 3–6 white eggs, incubated by female for 13–17 days. Nestlings cared for by both parents; fledge at 18–25 days, but can climb about on bankside, and swim and dive well before they can fly.

LIFESTYLE: The five species in the dipper family (two in Europe and Asia, two in South America, and the North American dipper) share a very similar structure and lifestyle. These are the only really aquatic members of the perching-bird order (Passeriformes). Their closest relatives are probably the thrushes.

The North American dipper is superbly adapted to feeding underwater. As it perches on a boulder in midstream, it frequently submerges its head to search for

EYE SIGNALS
When it blinks, the flash
of the dipper's white
eyelids acts as a signal
of alarm, aggression,
or excitement.

prey. It then walks, flies, swims, or dives into the water, using its strong, sturdy feet to grip tightly onto streambed rocks and avoid being swept away by the current. They even "fly" underwater, with powerful wingbeats.

Other adaptations include scales closing the bird's nostrils to stop water entering and extra hemoglobin in the blood to carry more oxygen for diving. Features helping the dipper survive very cold water are its extra downy plumage, with twice as many feathers as that of other similar-sized perching birds, and a metabolism that slows down on entering the water.

The dipper is named for its curious habit of bobbing, or dipping, its body up and down as if on springs. No-one knows the reason for this.

WINTER WREN

Troglodytes troglodytes
Family: TROGLODYTIDAE
Order: PASSERIFORMES

DISTRIBUTION: Breeds throughout temperate regions of the northern hemisphere, from Europe and North Africa to Asia, Japan, Alaska, central and southern Canada, and parts of the eastern United States. Northern populations winter farther south.

SIZE: Length 3.5in (9cm); weight 0.3–0.5oz (8–13g).

APPEARANCE: Very small, plump, active bird with distinctive short, upturned tail and spikelike bill. Upper parts and wings reddish-brown, barred with darker brown; underparts buffish-brown. Pale eyebrow. Blackish-brown bill, paler below; dark brown eyes; pinkish-brown legs.

DIET: Insects, spiders, and other small invertebrates.

BREEDING: In spring and summer. Male makes several domed nests of leaves, grasses, and mosses, in low-growing vegetation, a rock or wall crevice, or an abandoned bird's nest. The female chooses which nest to use. 5–8 white eggs, sometimes with tiny spots or speckles of black or reddish-brown, incubated by female for 14–17 days. Chicks cared for by both parents. Young fledge at 15–20 days. Often has 2 broods a year.

LIFESTYLE: Restless, busy, and amazingly noisy for such a tiny bird, the winter wren is one of the most common and successful small songbirds over much of its wide range. It usually draws attention to itself by its loud scolding calls and explosive, warbling song, but is not always easy to spot as it forages among, low, dense vegetation.

It has a creeping, mouselike manner, and flies low and fast on whirring wings before diving back into cover. It usually hunts alone, but at night many may roost together for warmth in cold weather. In mild winters many

FEARLESS DEFENDER
The tiny winter wren is surprisingly bold and even aggressive, often scolding people who come too close to its perch before diving out of sight into a thornbush or thicket.

populations stay on or near their breeding territories, but in harder weather they move south. In some more southerly U.S. states the birds appear only in winter, which accounts for their name. Elsewhere the species is often known as the northern wren. Males sing loudly to defend their territories. They may mate with more than one female, but each male makes several "cock's nests" even if he has only one mate. The female then selects one of the nests, lines it with feathers and lays her eggs, and the other nests are usually abandoned. Winter wrens can suffer in very cold winters, becoming locally rare, but their rapid breeding rate allows them to recover within a few years.

169

NORTHERN MOCKINGBIRD

> *Mimus polyglottos*
> Family: MIMIDAE
> Order: PASSERIFORMES

DISTRIBUTION: Farmland, open woodland, streamside thickets, desert scrub, as well as gardens and lawns in suburbs and towns, where it is common in North America, from southern Canada to Mexico and Caribbean islands; introduced to Hawaii and Bermuda.

SIZE: Length 9–11in (23–28cm); weight 1.3–2oz (36.2–55.7g).

APPEARANCE: Thrush-sized bird with sharp-pointed, slightly downcurved bill, short, rounded wings and long, tapered tail. Upperparts gray; wings blackish with two big white wing patches; underparts whitish; tail blackish, with white outer feathers; legs and bill gray; eyes pale yellow. Juvenile browner, buff with brown streaks below, with brownish eyes.

DIET: Fruits, berries, seeds and insects.

BREEDING: In spring and early summer. Pair builds cup nest of twigs, stems, other plant material and debris, lined with grasses, rootlets and hair or plant down, quite low down in shrub or tree. 3–6 pale blue or greenish eggs, marked with shades of reddish-brown, red and pale lilac; incubated by female for 11–14 days. Both parents care for young, which fledge at 12–14 days. Rears 2 (sometimes 3 or 4) broods a year.

LIFESTYLE: The northern mockingbird is justly famed for its song. This is reflected in both its common name and its scientific name, which means "mimic of many tongues". It is able to imitate song-phrases or calls of up to 30 or more other bird species. It repeats these in quick succession, interspersing them with expert mimicry of various other sounds, from barking dogs to saws or squeaking hinges, and its own liquid, warbling phrases and grating or squeaking notes. Each male has a repertoire of 150–300 phrases, repeated the same way every time it sings. It usually delivers this virtuoso performance from a prominent perch, continuing from before dawn to evening and often into moonlit nights. Unusually, females as well as males sing in fall to establish feeding territories. Mockingbirds are fierce defenders of their nesting territories. They will attack intruders, not only rivals of its own species but other birds, including crows and bald eagles. It will even launch a spirited attack on a marauding cat.

When a mockingbird chases insects on the ground, it often raises and lowers its wings to flash their broad white patches. This may serve to startle its prey, making them easier to snap up. Flashing the wing-patches is also a feature of mockingbird territorial displays.

GROUND-DWELLER
With its upright posture, strong legs, and long balancing tail, the northern mockingbird is well suited to a life spent mostly running or hopping on the ground.

DUNNOCK

Prunella modularis
Family: PRUNELLIDAE
Order: PASSERIFORMES

DISTRIBUTION: Breeds and feeds in woodlands, parks, gardens, heaths, and scrublands throughout Europe, Asia Minor, Iran, and the Caucasus. Some winter farther south in the Mediterranean and limited numbers in northern Africa.

SIZE: Length 5.5in (14cm); weight 0.5–0.9oz (13–26g).

APPEARANCE: Inconspicuous and small, bird, mainly reddish-brown, streaked with black. Head, breast, and throat bluish-gray, except for brownish cheek patch and streaked brown crown; narrow buff wing-bar. Pinkish-brown legs, blackish-brown bill, and brown eyes.

DIET: Mainly insects, spiders, and worms; also seeds.

BREEDING: Has variety of mating arrangements, from pairs to groups of males and females, formed from early spring. Nest is a stout cup of twigs, stems, roots, dry leaves, and moss, lined with hair and wool.

3–6 deep blue eggs, incubated by female for 12–13 days. Chicks cared for by both parents, plus other adults if present; fledge at 12 days. 1–3 broods each year.

LIFESTYLE: Although it looks very like a female sparrow, the dunnock is one of a small family known as the accentors. It is an unobtrusive little bird that typically forages on the ground, creeping beneath overhanging foliage with a jerky, mouselike shuffle. Its retiring habits give no clue to its extraordinary mating system, which can involve almost any combination of two, three, or four males and females, and sometimes even more.

Male and female dunnocks claim their own territories, although they often overlap. Frequently a male attracts a single female by singing and chasing displays, and the two form a pair. But he often manages to mate with more than one female – and on her part, a female tries to mate with extra males. The original male tries to prevent this by guarding her closely, and pecking at her vent to make her eject any sperm from another male before mating. But a male cannot be sure which chicks are his, and both may end up feeding the brood in the belief that they are raising their own young. Since each male may have more than one mate, the situation can get very complicated.

UNUSUAL MATING BEHAVIOR Male and female dunnocks are hard to tell apart. Both seek multi-partner matings that may be unique among birds.

FIRECREST

Regulus ignicapillus
Family: REGULIDAE
Order: PASSERIFORMES

DISTRIBUTION: Breeds in woods, hedges, parks, and gardens from western and central Europe, North Africa, Madeira, and Canary Islands to Asia Minor and Black Sea. Northern populations winter farther south.

SIZE: Length 3.5in (9cm); weight 0.2–0.3oz (4.5–8.2g).

APPEARANCE: Tiny warbler. Upperparts yellowish-green, with two whitish wingbars; white-tipped tail feathers. Male has bright orange-red crest, bordered by two black stripes that meet across forehead. Female has lemon-yellow crest. Pale grayish-brown throat and breast; white belly; brown legs. Black bill and brown eyes.

DIET: Insects and their larvae, plus spiders, many of minute size.

BREEDING: Starts in May: pair build deep, thick hammock-like nest of mosses, lichens, and spiders' webs, lined with feathers. 7–10 white to pale buff eggs, with fine pale brownish speckles, incubated by female for 14–17 days. Young cared for by both parents; fledge at 16–21 days.

LIFESTYLE: The high-pitched "tseet" call of the firecrest can often be heard in woodland throughout much of Europe, but the bird itself can be hard to see as it forages among the foliage high above the ground. Tiny and very agile, it slips through the leaves with short hops and often hovers to pick aphids and other small insects from beneath the leaves. It flits from tree to tree on whirring wings, rarely traveling far. Sometimes it feeds lower down in scrub, when it can be very tame; at close range its bold head stripes distinguish it from its close relative, the similar, but slightly smaller goldcrest.

In summer it can find all it needs within a small area, but in winter it often joins nomadic parties of tits

SHARP HEADGEAR
Although small and often hard to see, the firecrest has a bold head pattern. Only the male has the fiery orange-red crest; the female's is a more restrained shade of yellow.

and other small birds, which roam through the woods looking for food. Firecrests that breed in northern and eastern Europe cannot survive the harsh continental winters, so they migrate south and west to regions with milder climates, from southern Britain to France, Spain, Italy, Greece, and North Africa. They fly by night, covering surprising distances for such tiny, weak-flying birds.

In spring the male firecrest advertises for a mate with a sharp, accelerating "zi zi zi zezezeeee" song, and displays to any responsive females by pointing his bill at them to show off his head stripes and brilliant crest color. The pairs nest in a variety of mixed woodlands, and even in large gardens, favoring conifer trees such as spruce where their nests are well concealed in the foliage.

PIED FLYCATCHER

Ficedula hypoleuca
Family: MUSCICAPIDAE
Order: PASSERIFORMES

DISTRIBUTION: Open forests and woodland, parkland, and gardens, from western Europe and northwest Africa to western Asia. Winters in tropical Africa.

SIZE: Length 5in (13cm); weight 0.3–0.5oz (10–14g).

APPEARANCE: Compact, rounded, short-tailed bird with quite short bill. Breeding male has mainly black upperparts, often grayer on nape, shoulders, and rump; broad white wingbar; white outer tail feathers; white splash or spots on forehead; and white underparts. Female similar but brown instead of black, with smaller wingbar, darker forehead and off-white underparts. Non-breeding male molts to brown, resembling female. Black legs and bill; brown eyes.

DIET: Insects and spiders; also worms and berries in the fall.

BREEDING: In summer. Female builds loose cup nest of grasses, leaves, roots, and other pliable plant material, lined with grass and hair, in tree hole, wall crevice, or nestbox. 4–7 pale blue eggs, incubated by female for 12–13 days; male typically brings food. Chicks fledge at 13–16 days.

LIFESTYLE: Flycatchers get their name from their characteristic hunting technique of making brief sallies to snatch flies and other winged insects out of the air. Many hunt from favorite perches, where they wait for suitable victims to fly within range. The pied flycatcher is more mobile, and rarely returns to the same perch after seizing a victim. It also searches for prey among twigs and leaves, or even from the ground, sometimes picking them from the foliage while hovering. It spends a lot of time in dense cover, briefly flitting out to intercept insects before disappearing again. When perching in the open, it often attracts attention by flicking its wings and dipping its tail.

Pied flycatchers winter in the tropics, like many insect-eating birds, and many fall migrants head west to fatten up in Spain and Portugal before passing over the Strait of Gibraltar into Africa. When they return north in spring they sometimes have problems finding suitable nesting sites. Many of the best tree holes are claimed by resident small birds such as tits before the flycatchers arrive, and this may inhibit breeding in

some areas. The birds take readily to nestboxes, however, and if plenty of these are provided in suitable woodland the local pied flycatcher population can increase dramatically. Where plenty of nest sites are available, a paired male may start a second family with another female on a separate territory. He then returns to help feed the first brood while the second female is incubating her clutch of eggs.

FLASH COLOR
The white wing patches of the male show up brightly against the bird's mainly black plumage as it darts out of cover to seize an insect in mid-air.

EASTERN BLUEBIRD

Sialia sialis
Family: TURDIDAE
Order: PASSERIFORMES

DISTRIBUTION: Breeds in open country with scattered trees, forest edges, clearings, gardens and parks from east Canada through USA east of Rockies to Gulf coast, western Mexico, and Honduras. Northern populations winter farther south.

SIZE: Length 5.5–7.5in (14–19cm); weight 1.1oz (31.6g).

APPEARANCE: Small, plump-bodied; males have deep blue upperparts, with chestnut throat, sides of neck, breast and flanks; wings tipped with black; belly white; bill gray; legs dark brown; eyes dark brown. Females are similar but duller.

DIET: Insects (such as crickets, grasshoppers, beetles, larvae), earthworms, and fruit. It catches most of its insect and other prey on the ground. It also gleans invertebrates from foliage, and snatches flying insects in mid-air in a brief flight from a low perch.

BREEDING: In spring, pair builds loose cup nest of dry grasses, stems and small twigs, lined with grasses, in tree hole, hollow post, old nest, or nestbox. 3–7 pale blue (sometimes white) eggs, incubated by both parents, mainly female, for 12–16 days. Chicks cared for by both parents who feed their young mainly on insects. Fledge at 15–20 days, but often remain with male while female starts second brood. May produce three broods a year.

LIFESTYLE: During courtship, the brightly colored male flutters in front of the female on half-open wings, his tail fanned, as he pours out his brief but musical warbling song. This is an elaboration of the bird's usual call, a musical *chur-lee* with a rising inflection.

In recent times, the eastern bluebird has suffered serious declines in many areas. This was largely because of many suitable nest holes being taken by starlings and house sparrows. Both are Old World species introduced to North America from the 19th century onwards that became common and successful, and are aggressive rivals with native hole-nesters for natural nesting sites.

Conservationists concerned at the bluebirds' plight reacted by erecting specially designed nestboxes, and monitored sites to keep the competing starlings and sparrows away. Providing this help has paid off in many cases, and has resulted in a comeback of these much-loved, colorful birds.

FARMER'S FRIEND
In its lifetime, an eastern bluebird will eat huge numbers of insects and their larvae, including many harmful to agriculture. In winter bluebirds eagerly devour wild berries.

EUROPEAN ROBIN

Erithacus rubecula
Family: TURDIDAE
Order: PASSERIFORMES

DISTRIBUTION: Breeds in forests, woodlands, parks, and gardens from western Europe and North Africa to western Siberia and Iran.

SIZE: Length 5.5in (14cm); weight 0.5–0.8oz (14–22g).

APPEARANCE: Small, plump, robust with olive-brown upperparts and orange-red forehead, throat, and breast, bordered by grayish-blue band. Brown legs, bill, and eyes.

DIET: Insects, insect larvae, spiders and worms.

BREEDING: In spring the female builds a sturdy cup nest of dead leaves, grasses, and moss, lined with hair and fine roots, in hollow log, tree trunk, stump, bank, or low shrub. 5–6 white eggs, spotted, speckled and faintly blotched with light brown or pinkish-buff,

RED FOR DANGER
When defending its territory against an intruder, a European robin cocks its tail, throws its head up and puffs out its bright red breast, while singing with oddly strained notes.

incubated by female for 12–15 days while male brings food. Chicks cared for by both parents; fledge at 12–15 days. May have 2 or 3 broods a year.

LIFESTYLE: Throughout most of its range the European robin is a bird of forest edges and open woods, where it follows large animals as they search for food and snatches any insects or other small creatures that they expose in the process.

It is particularly associated with wild boar, which dig and churn up the soil with their snouts. In Britain – where wild boar are extinct – it has transferred its allegiance to human gardeners cultivating the soil. In the process it has become very tame, but over most of Europe it remains shy and elusive.

Robins are solitary for most of the year, and unusually both sexes sing and defend territories outside the breeding season. Each bird often returns to the same winter territory every year, a habit that has endeared the "robin redbreast" to the designers and buyers of Christmas cards.

In spring and summer each mated pair defends a joint territory, with the male responsible for patrolling its boundaries. Neighboring males often engage in competitive singing from nearby perches, filling the air with a rich, varied, musical warbling, but if this fails to keep the rivals apart they will fight. Usually they avoid actual physical contact, but if neither male backs down they may peck at each other until one bird is killed.

SONG THRUSH

Turdus philomelos
Family: TURDIDAE
Order: PASSERIFORMES

DISTRIBUTION: Breeds in a variety of woodlands, farmland with hedges, and gardens, from Scandinavia, western Europe, and North Africa to western Siberia and Iraq. Northern populations move south for the winter.

SIZE: Length 9in (23cm); weight 2–3.5oz (57–100g).

APPEARANCE: Compact, relatively small thrush with upright stance. Warm brown upperparts; creamy-white underparts, spotted with dark brown; buffish-orange tinge on breast and flanks; whitish chin. Golden-brown underwings show in flight. Pinkish legs; golden-brown bill, darker at tip; light brown eyes.

DIET: Worms, snails, and insects, especially caterpillars; also fruits in the fall.

BREEDING: In spring and summer. Female builds cup nest of grasses, twigs, roots, dead leaves, mosses, and lichens, lined with wood pulp or mud, in tree, shrub, or building, up to 12 feet (3.7m) above ground. 4–6 light blue eggs, sparsely spotted, speckled, or blotched with black or purplish-brown, incubated by female for 11–15 days. Chicks fledge at 12–16 days.

LIFESTYLE: The song thrush is well named, for it sings loudly through most of the year, using repeated phrases and often mimicking other birds. It is a familiar garden bird over much of its range, usually foraging alone with a characteristic habit of pausing with its head cocked to one side, as if listening for prey. It eats a lot of snails, especially in very dry or cold weather when other prey is scarce, smashing their shells open by beating them against a rock with its bill. It then pulls the snail's body free of the shell fragments and wipes it against the ground before eating it. The scattered fragments are left where they fall.

In regions with mild winters, song thrushes may stay on or near their breeding territories throughout the year, and start singing in the fall to reassert their ownership. In colder parts of their range they migrate south for the winter in large, loose flocks, returning in spring to pair up and claim new territories. Severe winters in Europe may cause large-scale movements into North Africa.

Although most song thrush populations have stayed stable, numbers have declined steeply in Britain and the Netherlands since the mid-1970s. The decline has probably been caused by changing farming methods, particularly the use of pesticides that kill slugs and snails. It is possible that these not only reduce the prey supply, but also cause longterm poisoning.

SNAIL ANVILS
Song thrushes often use favorite "anvils" to smash snail shells. In gardens they use rocks, paving slabs, and even concrete steps, which become littered with shell fragments.

BLUE TIT

Parus caeruleus
Family: PARIDAE
Order: PASSERIFORMES

DISTRIBUTION: Resident in variety of woodlands, parks, and gardens, from southern Scandinavia, western Europe, North Africa, and the Canary Islands to the Volga river and parts of the Middle East.

SIZE: Length 4.5in (11.5cm); weight 0.3–0.5oz (9–14g).

APPEARANCE: Small, plump bird with longish tail. Grayish-blue upperparts with yellowish-green shoulders, cobalt blue crown, white forehead, cheeks, and nape patch, black eyestripe, and black collar on nape, linking with black bib; sulfur-yellow underparts. Some races have darker heads. Dark slate-blue legs; black bill; dark brown eyes.

DIET: Insects and their larvae; also buds, fruits, nuts, and seeds.

BREEDING: In spring and early summer. Female builds cup nest of grasses, dead leaves, mosses, hair, and spiders' webs, lined with hair and feathers, in hole in tree or wall, or in nestbox. 7–12 white eggs, finely speckled or blotched with purplish-red or reddish-brown, incubated by female for 12–16 days while male brings food. Chicks are cared for by both parents; fledge at 15–23 days.

LIFESTYLE: Common in a wide variety of habitats throughout its basically European range, the blue tit is an adaptable opportunist with a talent for making the most of local and seasonal food sources. It takes a wide variety of natural foods, from insects and spiders to pollen and nectar, picking edible items from twigs and leaves as it forages though trees and shrubs. It is extremely acrobatic, often hanging upside-down to get at food. It has learned to make the most of backyard feeders, where its agility makes it a favorite. Up to 200 blue tits may visit a well-supplied feeder in a single day, and the species is very common in suburban gardens

MORE YELLOW THAN BLUE
The blue plumage of a mature male blue tit is particularly bright during the breeding season, but for much of the year the bird's yellow breast is more conspicuous.

and even in built-up cities. In Britain for example it has also learned to raid doorstep deliveries of foil-capped milk bottles for their cream – a celebrated example of learning among birds. Outside the breeding season blue tits forage in flocks, often with other tit species. Despite this the pairs often persist from year to year, claiming new breeding territories in spring. They often use nestboxes, laying large clutches of eggs. The hatching of the chicks is timed to coincide with the spring flush of juicy caterpillars, and the adults are kept very busy catching and carrying this protein-rich food to their hungry young. Finding enough caterpillars is rarely a problem for woodland nesters, but blue tits that nest in backyard nestboxes often have problems feeding their large broods of young, partly because many caterpillars are destroyed by garden pesticides.

LONG-TAILED TIT

Aegithalos caudatus
Family: AEGITHALIDAE
Order: PASSERIFORMES

DISTRIBUTION: Lives in woodlands, scrublands and parks from Scandinavia and western Europe across Asia to Japan, to altitudes of 9,000ft (2,740m). Populations that breed in the far north may winter farther south.

SIZE: Length 5.5in (14cm); weight 0.3–0.4oz (7.5–10g).

APPEARANCE: Small, rounded bird with long tail and very small black bill. Upper parts black or gray; primary feathers blackish-brown, inner primaries edged with white; tail blackish or dark gray. Blackish triangle from shoulders to just above tail; pinkish flanks; white underparts. Some races have pure white heads, others have black or grayish eyestripe.

DIET: Small insects; some seeds.

BREEDING: From March to April, pairs build oval domed nests of moss bound with spider webs and hair, coated with lichens and lined with feathers, in low, often thorny bushes or brambles, or beside tree trunk or in large fork, up to 70 ft (20 m) above ground. 8–12 white eggs, sometimes finely speckled with purplish-red, incubated mainly by female for 12–14 days; male brings food. Chicks cared for by both parents; fledge at 14–18 days.

LIFESTYLE: Resembling a fluffy pink ball on a stick – the "stick" being its long, slender tail – the long-tailed tit is an active, agile bird that typically feeds in shrubs and trees. It is sociable for most of the year, traveling through the woods in family parties or larger flocks, picking tiny insects, spiders and their eggs from the bark, buds, and foliage. The feeding parties have a characteristic habit of moving from tree to tree one at a time, or in single file across larger gaps, calling constantly with short, sharp calls and a high, nasal "tzee-tzee-tzee" to stay in contact.

ISLAND RACE
Although instantly
recognizable, the long-tailed
tit has several distinct
races. This is the British
race, with a dark band
above its eye; birds from
continental northern Europe
have all-white heads.

EURASIAN NUTHATCH

Sitta europaea
Family: SITTIDAE
Order: PASSERIFORMES

DISTRIBUTION: Woodlands, parks, and gardens from western Europe to Kamchatka (Siberia) and Japan.

SIZE: Length 4–5in (11–13cm); weight 0.7–0.8oz (20–24g).

APPEARANCE: Small, big-headed bird with strong, pointed, slate-gray bill and short, square tail.

HEAD-FIRST
Unlike other birds a nuthatch nearly always descends a tree head-first, keeping a tight grip on the bark with its claws. It never uses its tail as a prop, like a woodpecker.

Bluish-gray upperparts, with black eyestripe extending to side of neck; the Eurasian nuthatch has a white throat and chestnut flanks. Underparts range from white in northern birds to deep chestnut-yellow in southern populations. Yellowish-brown legs; dark grayish-brown eyes.

DIET: Mainly insects in summer, mostly taken from tree bark; also seeds and nuts in fall and winter.

BREEDING: In spring, female builds a loose cup nest of dead leaves and pieces of bark in a tree hole, wall crevice, or nestbox, and lays 6–9 white eggs, spotted, speckled, and blotched with shades of red, brown, and purple. Eggs incubated by female only for 14–18 days, while male brings food. Chicks fledge at 23–25 days.

LIFESTYLE: The nuthatches are a very distinctive family of 25 species, all sharing the same compact, dumpy, sharp-billed, short-tailed form; the Eurasian nuthatch is one of the most widespread. Like all its kind it is specialized for feeding on large trees, climbing up, over, and under their trunks and branches with a jerky motion, while clinging on with its strong, sharp claws. Lively and noisy, it probes crevices and chisels into soft wood in search of insects and their grubs, but during spring and summer it often abandons its bark-searching in favor of picking caterpillars from foliage. When insects become scarce in the fall it turns to seeds and nuts, often wedging them into bark crevices so it can hammer them open with its strong bill. The hammering sound is often audible from some distance.

Pairs of nuthatches often defend a joint territory against neighboring nuthatches throughout the year, foraging for food only within their patch of woodland. In spring the male sings to reassert his ownership of the territory, drawing himself upright to produce a series of loud whistles. Once the pair has found a suitable nest site – often an old woodpecker hole – the female plasters mud around the entrance to reduce its size and deny access to bigger birds. They are aggressive towards great spotted woodpeckers, which sometimes steal their young, although since the woodpeckers typically excavate new holes each year the two species do not compete for nesting sites.

BROWN TREECREEPER

Climacteris picumnus
Family: CLIMACTERIDAE
Order: PASSERIFORMES

DISTRIBUTION: In drier, fairly open forests, woods and scrub, with tree-stumps and fallen branches, often by rivers and lakes; common in much of eastern Australia.

SIZE: Length 6.3–7in (16–18cm); weight about 0.7–1oz (20–30g).

APPEARANCE: Small, with slender, downcurved bill and proportionately large, strong legs and feet; upperparts brown (blackish in Cape York race), with gray head and neck, buff eyebrow (white in Cape York race), dark patch through eye; upper breast gray, with patch of fine streaks in center, black in male, reddish-brown in female; pale buff streaks, edged with black, on lower breast, flanks and belly; under tail coverts have barred black-and-white pattern; pale buff wing-band in flight.

DIET: Insects, especially ants.

BREEDING: May-December, mostly between June and January,

depending on location; cup-shaped nest, built by both members of the pair, of grass, lined with feathers, hair or fur, with base built up of grass or the dung of animals such as horses, cattle or kangaroos; sited in a tree hollow, stump or fence post near the ground. 2–3 pink eggs, heavily marked with red and purple streaks and freckles; incubation 16–18 days; young fledge in 25–26 days.

LIFESTYLE: This soberly plumaged little gray and brown bird was nicknamed "woodpecker" for its tree-climbing lifestyle. However, it is not related to the woodpeckers; indeed, Australia is one of the few major areas in the world where there are no woodpeckers. The Australian treecreepers do not seem to be closely related to the northern hemisphere treecreepers of Europe, Asia, and North America, either; it is more likely that they evolved a remarkably similar lifestyle independently. Like their northern counterparts, the brown treecreeper and the five other species of Australian treecreepers have extremely distinctive feeding behavior. They climb a tree-trunk in spirals, with jerky, mouselike movements, pecking at or probing into the bark for insects as they go, and often continue along the upper branches. When they reach the top of the tree, they glide down to the base of another nearby tree. Unlike northern hemisphere treecreepers, brown treecreepers often feed on the ground or on fallen timber, too.

Brown treecreepers live in pairs or groups of up to six individuals, usually made up of a breeding pair and the couple's male offspring, who help feed female and young.

NATURAL CLIMBER
The brown treecreeper is well adapted for its tree-climbing lifestyle, with long, strong claws on large, powerful feet, with which it can cling tightly to the bark.

CHESTNUT-FLANKED WHITE-EYE

Zosterops erythropleurus
Family: ZOSTEROPIDAE
Order: PASSERIFORMES

DISTRIBUTION: Breeds in forests, open woodlands, groves and thickets in extreme southeast Russia, Manchuria, North Korea and northeast China. Winters in Indo-China, in woodland and scrub.

SIZE: Length 4.5in (11.5cm); weight 9.9–11.5g (0.3–0.4oz).

THE EYES HAVE IT
Along with most other members of its family, this neat little bird has distinctive, fine, silky white feathers around its eyes. This feature gave the white-eyes their common name.

APPEARANCE: Very small bird with rounded wings, a sharply pointed, slightly downcurved bill, short legs. Upperparts, wings and tail bright yellowish-green; throat yellow; breast gray-white; belly and eye-ring white; flanks usually chestnut; undertail yellow.

DIET: Mainly insects, nectar, pollen, berries and other fruit.

BREEDING: In summer. Pairs for life. Builds cup nest in well-concealed tree fork. 2–6 whitish or pale blue eggs, incubated by both parents for 11–12 days. Chicks cared for by both parents; fledge at 11 days.

LIFESTYLE: The chestnut-flanked white-eye roams forests and woods in small flocks, often together with other species of small perching birds. Members of a flock keep in touch with one another as they travel by uttering plaintive, high-pitched contact calls. Like other white-eyes, chestnut-flanked white-eyes are agile and restless. They are active feeders, usually hunting for small insects and spiders and picking them off the foliage of the tree canopy and scrub layer. Sometimes they catch flying insects in mid-air. Like other white-eyes, they also eat fruit juices, fruit pulp, pollen and nectar, sucking up these energy-rich foods with the aid of a comb-like tip to the tongue.

To defend its territory or a food source against a rival, a chestnut-flanked white-eye will erect its conspicuous, bright white eye-ring feathers. It may add to its threatening appearance by spreading its wings and rapidly quivering them and clattering its beak to expose its yellow inside. Males have a melodious, rich, warbling song.

The 90 or so species of small warbler-like birds in the white-eye family are widespread in the woodlands of Africa, southern Asia and Australia. The great majority live in the tropics and subtropics, but a few species are found farther south or, like the chestnut-flanked white-eye, breed farther north. Many species are isolated on remote islands.

Little is known of the chestnut-flanked white-eye's current status, As it is tied to woodlands of various sorts throughout the year, it is likely to be affected by logging in both its breeding and wintering ranges, but its versatile feeding habits are an advantage.

NORTHERN CARDINAL

Cardinalis cardinalis
Family: CARDINALIDAE
Order: PASSERIFORMES

DISTRIBUTION: Woodland edges, copses, thickets, parks and gardens of North and Central America, from southeastern Canada to northern Guatemala and Belize; introduced to Hawaii and Bermuda.

SIZE: Length 8–9in (20.5–23cm); weight 1.2–2.3oz (33.6–64.9g).

APPEARANCE: Plump, starling-sized bird with heavy, cone-shaped bill, tall, pointed crest on head, and longish tail. Male red, with front of face and throat black. Legs brown; bill pinkish; eyes brown. Female has greenish-brown upperparts, tinged with red on crest, wings, and tail; underparts pinkish-brown; face and throat pattern fainter, dusky gray. Juvenile browner overall, with grayish bill, juvenile female lacks red tones.

DIET: Insects, seeds, fruit, flowers, buds, tree sap (left over from the boring of woodpeckers called sapsuckers).

BREEDING: In spring. Female builds cup nest of twigs, stems, grasses, bark, rootlets and vines mixed with other plant material and debris such as paper; lined with fine grasses, rootlets, lichens, or hair. 2–5 grayish-, bluish- or greenish-white eggs, spotted, speckled and blotched with brown and pale purple or gray; incubated by female for 11–13 days; males feeds her. Chicks cared for by both parents. Usually has 2 or 3 broods a year, sometimes 4 broods. Male cares for first brood while his mate incubates her next clutch of eggs. Leave nest at 9–11 days; fledge by 19 days; become independent at 38–45 days.

LIFESTYLE: Named for the red robes worn by Roman Catholic cardinals, this attractive bird is a familiar visitor to surburban bird-

SEED CRACKER
The northern cardinal's big, cone-shaped bill, powered by well-developed jaw muscles, enables this beautiful bird to crack open the hardest seeds.

feeders and city parks. It is an abundant North American breeder, steadily expanding its range northwards.

Although it may be quite wary of humans, the cardinal is a fierce defender of its territory and can also be very aggressive to other birds during competition for food.

Male and female court one another by singing softly while swaying their bodies from side to side, with their necks outstretched and crests held erect. The song, a series of rich, whistling notes, can be heard for much of the year, and the female sings as well as the male, though more quietly and not so often. She usually sings after her mate has established the nesting territory but before she lays her eggs. This probably serves to bond the pair and synchronize their reproductive states.

PAINTED BUNTING

Passerina ciris
Family: EMBERIZIDAE
Order: PASSERIFORMES

DISTRIBUTION: Woodland edges, low, often swampy thickets, streamside scrub, farmland and gardens of southern North America, with two separate populations, one down the southeast coast, and a much larger one further west, from southern Missouri south to northern Mexico. Winters from southern Florida and Gulf coast to Panama and Cuba.

SIZE: Length 5–5.5in (12.5–14cm); weight 0.5–0.7oz (12.9–19g).

APPEARANCE: Small, plump-bodied songbird with heavy, conical bill. Male multicolored, with underparts, shoulders and rump bright red, wings and tail duller reddish and greenish head, neck and cheeks violet-blue; back glossy green; bill yellowish-brown; eyes dark brown, with red eye-ring; legs dark brown. Female has green upperparts, dusky yellow to amber underparts and yellow eye-ring. Drab brown juvenile has distinctive traces of green above, yellow below.

DIET: Mainly seeds of grasses and weeds; also insects.

BREEDING: in spring and early summer. Female builds deep cup nest of grasses, stems and leaves, lined with hair and grasses, woven around supports in bush, vine or tangle of Spanish moss, high in tree. 3–5 whitish eggs, finely speckled with chestnut-red and purple; incubated by female for 11–12 days. Young cared for by both parents. Fledge at 12–14 days. May then be fed by male while female starts next brood. May have up to 4 broods a year.

LIFESTYLE: The male painted bunting is one of North America's most brilliantly colored birds. However, he is often surprisingly difficult to spot, because he is shy, spending much of his time hidden among dense cover outside the breeding season. Here, his complex colour pattern breaks up his outline.

In spring, males may be more obvious, especially when they perch on a prominent perch in full sunlight to sing and are revealed in all their glory. The song is an attractive series of clear, rich, warbling notes.

Unfortunately, the species is declining. The situation is especially serious in the east. Here, the birds are threatened for two main reasons. Firstly, the coastal and streamside habitats they inhabit are exposed to pressure from human development. Secondly, their nests are taken over by brown-headed cowbirds, recent arrivals that have expanded their range into the buntings' habitat. The cowbirds lay their eggs in the buntings' nests, to the detriment of the foster parents' offspring. Unlike the western birds, which have lived alongside the cowbirds for thousands of years, the eastern population has not had time to develop measures to reduce this parasitism, and suffers far more from its effects.

FRENCH NICKNAME
The male's lovely plumage earned the painted bunting the popular name *nonpareil*, French for "without equal." It also made it a popular cagebird until federal laws gave it protection.

Blue-headed Vireo

Vireo solitarius
Family: VIREONIDAE
Order: PASSERIFORMES

DISTRIBUTION: Breeds in mixed woodland, across Canada (eastern British Columbia east to Newfoundland) and south through eastern USA, from Minnesota east to Maine and south to northern Georgia. Winters in the southern USA and as far south as Cuba and Nicaragua.

SIZE: Length 5–6in (13–15cm); weight 0.5–0.75oz (15–21g).

APPEARANCE: Small, sturdy songbird. Head bluish-gray, with broad white eye-ring that extends as stripe to base of bill; back bright olive-green; wings blackish, with yellowish feather edges and 2 yellowish wingbars; underparts white; breast sides and flanks yellow, sometimes with faint greenish streaks; blackish tail, whitish on outer feathers; legs and bill dark gray; larger race found in Appalachians has a darker, grayer back and only the flanks yellow.

DIET: Insects and fruit.

BREEDING: In spring and summer. Both sexes build cup nest of bark, rootlets, grasses, lichens, mosses, feathers, plant down and debris, bound together with spider webs, attached to twigs around rim; lined with grasses, mosses, hair or fur. 3–5 white or creamy eggs, sparsely spotted or speckled with brown, chestnut or black, incubated by both parents, for 10–13 days. Chicks fledge at 11–13 days.

LIFESTYLE: Vireos are quite similar to wood warblers, but more heavily built, bigger headed and less active. Also, they have thicker bills with a slight hook at the tip. They feed mainly on insects among the foliage in spring and summer; blue-headed vireos eat a wide range, from bugs, beetles, wasps and dragonflies, to moths and their caterpillars. In autumn and winter, they eat large amounts of a variety of fruit, such as the berries of dogwood and viburnum.

COWBIRD INVADERS
This vireo is often host
to cowbirds that lay
their eggs in its nest.
The vireo feeds the
bigger cowbird young at
the expense of its own.

Blue-eyed vireos are often remarkably tame and fearless of humans when incubating eggs. They have allowed people to feed them, stroke them or even gently lift them up. Despite this, they are generally unobtrusive, leading a mainly solitary life in the treetops outside the breeding season.

The blue-headed vireo is one of a group of three very closely related species, the others being Cassin's vireo of western North America and the plumbeous vireo of south-western USA, Mexico and northern Central America. All were formerly regarded as races of a single species, called the solitary vireo. They share similar shape, habits and calls, but show subtle differences in plumage and song. The male blue-headed vireo's song is a series of short, rich, phrases, with quite long pauses between each phrase, contrasting with the hoarser songs of its relatives.

AMERICAN GOLDFINCH

Carduelis tristis
Family: FRINGILLIDAE
Order: PASSERIFORMES

DISTRIBUTION: Open woodlands, roadsides, weedy fields and gardens in North America, breeding from southern Canada to as far south as Baja California, northern Mexico, and central Georgia. Most central and northwestern populations move south and southeast to winter in eastern and western parts of breeding range; some travel well into Mexico.

SIZE: Length 4.5–5.5in (11.5–14cm); weight 0.3–0.7oz (8.6–20.7g).

APPEARANCE: Small bird with short, conical bill. Male in breeding plumage bright yellow, with black cap, black wings with flight feathers edged with white and white wingbar; tail black-and-white; rump and undertail white; legs pinkish-brown; bill yellowish-brown; eyes brown; non-breeding male brownish, lacking dark cap. Female has dull olive back and head, yellow underparts; she is brown with grayish-brown underparts in winter.

DIET: Mainly seeds, some insects, occasionally buds and berries.

BREEDING: In spring and summer. Nest a cup of tightly woven plant fibers, bark and wool, bound with spider webs and lined with plant down, well off ground in tree or shrub. 4–6 pale bluish or greenish-blue eggs, incubated by female for 12–14 days. Chicks fledge at 11–17 days.

LIFESTYLE: Widespread and common, this little finch is nick-named the "wild canary" for its attractive, canary-like song and breeding coloration. It also has a distinctive, sweet, twittering, "just-look-at-me" contact call, often heard from birds as they take to the wing with their dancing, strongly undulating flight.

American goldfinches are gregarious birds, usually seen in pairs, family groups or, after breeding, in large flocks. These often also contain other finches, such as pine siskins, common redpolls, and arctic redpolls.

Over most of its range, the American goldfinch is a late nester, ensuring its young hatch in late summer and autumn, when there are plenty of suitable soft weed seeds, such as those of thistles, sunflowers, and teasels. The parents feed their nestlings on a regurgitated milky pulp of seeds. The neat nest cup is woven so tightly that it would become filled with water during heavy rain if the sitting bird did not shield the young and prevent them from drowning.

GOOD PROVIDER
During the two-week incubation period, the male American goldfinch is kept very busy finding food for his mate, who may spend as much as 95 percent of her time on the nest.

PINE GROSBEAK

Pinicola enucleator
Family: FRINGILLIDAE
Order: PASSERIFORMES

DISTRIBUTION: Breeds mainly in open coniferous forests, especially spruce and larch, also in alder and birch forests; in winter also in deciduous woods, orchards, scrublands; wide range, across northern and western North America, and in Eurasia from northern Norway to far eastern Siberia and Hokkaido, north Japan.

SIZE: Length 8–10in (20–25.5cm); weight 1.58–2.2oz (43–62g).

APPEARANCE: Large, stout, long-bodied finch with longish forked tail and strong, stout, slightly hooked blackish bill. Male crimson to bright raspberry pink, with black mottling on back and "shoulders" and blackish wings and tail; two white wingbars; blackish eyestripe and often gray crescent below eye; lower belly white; legs, bill and eyes dark brown. Females and immature birds greenish-yellow to russet on head, back and rump, with grayish "shoulders" and belly, flanks, undertail and rump.

DIET: Seeds (especially of beech, also maples, crab apples and others), ash fruits, berries (particularly of rowan), spruce buds; also insects (mainly mosquitos) in summer.

BREEDING: In early summer. Female builds loose cup nest of twigs, lined with rootlets, grasses mosses and lichens. 3–5 blue-green eggs, spotted and blotched with black, purple and brown, incubated by female for 13–15 days; male brings food. Nestlings cared for by both parents; fledge at 13–20 days.

LIFESTYLE:
During the breeding season, the pine grosbeak is rather unobtrusive, preferring to remain hidden in foliage if approached. By contrast, feeding flocks in winter are often amazingly tame and very

easy to approach closely. Some populations make regular annual migrations, moving short distances to the south of their breeding range. Many birds, though, are normally resident – except in hard winters, when failures of wild seed and fruit crops force them much farther south than usual in search of food. At such times they may assemble in large numbers. These wanderers may visit towns to take advantage of berry-bearing shrubs or trees. These birds can be attracted to bird feeders with sunflower seeds.

ROLLER-COASTER FLIGHT
Like other finches, pine grosbeaks, such as this male, have a fast, bounding flight-style, alternating a burst of flapping upwards and a dive with closed wings.

EURASIAN GOLDFINCH

Carduelis carduelis
Family: FRINGILLIDAE
Order: PASSERIFORMES

DISTRIBUTION: Open woodland, scrubland, farmland, gardens, and waste ground from North Africa and western Europe to the Middle East and central Asia. Introduced to Australia and New Zealand.

SIZE: Length 5in (12cm); weight 0.5–0.6oz (14–17g).

REDHEAD
A female Eurasian goldfinch has marginally less red on her face than this male. She also has a slightly shorter bill, which makes her less able to extract seeds from prickly teasel seedheads.

APPEARANCE: Small, lightweight finch with sharp, pinkish-white bill. Tawny-brown upperparts, black wings with broad golden-yellow bars and white tips to primaries; black tail with white tip. Black crown and nape; broad white band behind each eye; bright crimson forehead, face, and upper chin. White rump and underparts; pale legs.

DIET: Small, half-ripe seeds of thistles and similar plants, plus insects and spiders in summer. The main threat to their survival is the use of weedkillers on farmland, since this destroys the thistles and other seed-producing plants that the goldfinches rely upon for food.

BREEDING: Spring to summer. Female builds cup nest of mosses, grasses, lichens, and roots, lined with plant down and wool. 4–6 pale blue eggs, finely spotted, speckled, streaked and blotched with purple, purplish-black, pink, or red at larger end. Incubation 12–14 days, by female; male brings food. Chicks are fed by both parents; fledge at 12–15 days; independent 1 week later. 2 or 3 broods a year.

LIFESTYLE: Some finches are heavyweight nutcrackers, with deep, powerful bills that can split cherry stones. The Eurasian goldfinch is the opposite: a slender, agile bird with a sharp-pointed bill that it uses like a precision instrument. It plucks soft, juicy, half-ripe seeds from the seedheads of thistles, burdocks, and similar tall composite "weeds," using its acrobatic skills to perch on the swaying stems as it feeds. It is the only European bird able to reach the seeds of teasels, which are protected by bristling spines; this gives it a valuable food source throughout the winter, when most of the more accessible seeds have been eaten. Where teasels are scarce it gathers the seeds of trees such as alder and birch.

From late summer to spring goldfinches forage in flocks or "charms," keeping in contact with musical, tinkling calls as they fly from one weed patch to another. In spring the big flocks break up as each mature male claims a breeding territory, defending it against rivals with his liquid, twittering song and performing dancing display flights. When the song attracts a female, the male courts her with swaying, wing-drooping displays that show off his bright golden-yellow wingbars.

ZEBRA FINCH

Poephila guttata
Family: ESTRILDIDAE
Order: PASSERIFORMES

DISTRIBUTION: Mainly in dry grasslands, scrub, open woodlands, edges of cultivation, saltmarshes, orchards, parks, gardens, always near water, throughout most of Australia, excluding most of the far north, east, south and Tasmania; also on the Lesser Sunda islands, Indonesia.

SIZE: Length 4in (10cm); weight about 0.3oz (9g).

APPEARANCE: Very small songbird with short, conical bill. Male has upperparts brownish-gray, grayer on crown; face has white band bordered with black from base of bill to cheeks, which are orange; chin to breast gray (Indonesian race) or finely barred pale gray and black (Australian race), separated from white belly by black border; flanks chestnut, with large white spots; rump white, tail black, overlapped at base by white-spotted black uppertail coverts; legs orange; bill and eyes orange to red. Female lacks orange cheeks and throat bars. Juvenile slightly duller than female, with black bill.

DIET: Grass seeds and shoots; also insects, including flying ants and termites.

BREEDING: Season variable; typically after rain. Builds untidy domed nest of twigs, grasses and rootlets, lined with plant down, wool, fur, and feathers, in low shrub or tree, fence post, or termite mound. Several pairs may nest in same tree. 4–7 pale blue or bluish-white eggs, incubated for 12–14 days by both sexes. Chicks cared for by both parents; fledge at about 3 weeks. May have several broods each year.

LIFESTYLE: Zebra finches are gregarious little birds, frequently forming large flocks – these may be huge, especially when birds from a wide area congregate at water-holes. They often drink several times a day, though they can survive for quite long periods without water if they have to.

Zebra finches may stay in the same area year-round, although in winter the flocks often live more nomadically, roaming to find enough food, and in years when there is drought, they wander about in search of water.

Tame and easy to approach, the zebra finch is a popular cagebird worldwide.

WATER SUCKERS
Zebra finches regularly visit water-holes and other places to drink. They do so in a similar manner to pigeons and doves, by dipping their bills in the water and sucking it up.

CHAFFINCH

Fringilla coelebs
Family: FRINGILLIDAE
Order: PASSERIFORMES

DISTRIBUTION: Breeds throughout Europe and extreme North Africa, in parts of western Asia, and east through Russia and Siberia to Lake Baikal region. Introduced to New Zealand and Cape Town area of South Africa.

SIZE: Length: 5.7in (14.5cm); weight: 0.7–0.8oz (20–24g)

APPEARANCE: Small, slim songbird with rounded head, small conical bill, and slight crest; fairly long tail with shallow fork. Breeding male has bluish crown and bill, pink cheeks, brown back, green rump, dark wings, and pink underparts. Female paler, mostly grayish-brown with darker back. Both sexes have white wingbars.

DIET: Mainly insects in breeding season; seeds and some berries during rest of year.

BREEDING: In spring and early summer. Builds neat cup nest of moss, lichen, and fibers bound with spiders' webs, lined with hair and feathers, in tree-fork or bush. 4–5 eggs, pale blue with dark spots; incubation 11–13 days, by female. Chicks fledge at 12–15 days. May raise 2 broods.

LIFESTYLE: Many finches are specialized for eating particular things, especially different sizes of seeds, but the chaffinch is a generalist, able to deal with a wide range of foods. This flexibility has made it very adaptable – a useful quality in a changing world. It feeds mainly on the ground, pecking up seeds with its stubby, all-purpose bill. Outside the breeding season it often swarms across farmland in large flocks, gathering spilt grain and other seeds.

Chaffinches may also collect food from trees and shrubs, especially in spring and summer when they eat a lot of caterpillars. They also feed these to their young – unlike most finches which feed their young mainly on seed paste. The high-protein diet gives the young a good start, which may be another reason why the chaffinch is so successful. Unlike other finches, chaffinches are also highly territorial, with a cheerful, rattling song that keeps rival males and their nests apart.

WINTER FLOCKS
In winter chaffinches tend to move south, and birds that breed in northern Asia vacate the whole region, migrating by day in large, conspicuous flocks to join residents farther south.

GOULDIAN FINCH

Erythrura gouldiae
Family: ESTRILDIDAE
Order: PASSERIFORMES

DISTRIBUTION: Open woodland away from human habitation, especially the edges of thickets and mangroves and dry savanna grassland; during the wet season, in scrubland and woodland with spinifex grasses; rarely far from water. Now occurs only in a few scattered areas of North Australia.

SIZE: Length 5–5.5in (12.5–14cm); weight 0.4–0.5oz (12–15g).

APPEARANCE: Neat, plump-bodied little songbird, with thick conical bill; brilliant multicolored plumage, especially in male, with a black or red face, black throat extending into a stripe along its bottom edge, a pale blue band running from the rear of the crown to separate the purple breast; yellow belly and flanks; upperparts grass-green, including long shoulder feathers overlying brownish wings; shortish black tail with long, pointed central feathers; pale pinkish or bone-colored bill, pale brownish legs,

dark eyes surrounded by white eye-ring. Female basically a duller version of male, with much shorter central tail feathers. Around 75 percent of adults have black heads, while almost 25 percent have red heads; there is also a very rare yellow-headed form. Juveniles much duller, with gray head and very short tail lacking elongated central feathers.

DIET: Grass seeds, other plant seeds, especially sorghum; also insects in the wet season.

BREEDING: January–April (wet season). Nest in tree hollow or hole in termite mound; 4–8 white eggs incubated for 12–13 days; young fledge in about 21 days.

LIFESTYLE: Until about 100 years ago, the Gouldian finch was a relatively common bird with a wide range in suitable habitat in Australia. Since then, populations

have suffered massive declines.
These are the result of two sorts
of impact by humans. The first was
large-scale trapping for the
lucrative cagebird trade, until the
practice was banned in late 1986.
More serious are changes to the
habitat, including burning of
grassland in the wet season by
farmers, which destroys nest sites,
shelter and food plants.

Today, there may be as few as
2,500 breeding adults left in the
world. Conservationists are
studying its precise needs in an
attempt to save this lovely bird.

POPULAR CAGEBIRD
With its gorgeous, rain-
bow-hued plumage, the
Gouldian finch is
extremely popular with
keepers and breeders
of aviary birds.

JAVA SPARROW

Padda oryzivora
Family: ESTRILDIDAE
Order: PASSERIFORMES

DISTRIBUTION: Native to the islands of Java and Bali, and the small island of Bawean, in Indonesia; introduced to or escaped from captivity in Africa, southern Asia, Hawaii, Florida, and many other places worldwide. Occurs mainly near human habitation and in farmland, but also in remote grassland or open woodland.

SIZE: Length 6–6.7in (15–17cm); weight about 1oz (30g).

APPEARANCE: A plump, sparrow-sized bird with a massive conical bill; head boldly marked, with a black cap and "necklace" contrasting with the white face and huge brilliant coral pink bill; most of rest of plumage, including throat, breast, upper belly, back, "shoulders," rump, and inner wings pale gray; flight feathers slightly darker gray; most of belly and flanks pale dull pinkish, undertail creamy-white; tail black; legs and feet pink; eyes blackish, surrounded by pink ring.

Juveniles are a much duller version of their parents, grayish brown (darker above), with a pale buffish face and a gray bill with pink paler and restricted to the base.

DIET: Mainly grass seeds, fruits and small insects, but also eats large amounts of rice and maize when available.

BREEDING: Season varies; in native range from April to August. Builds rounded nest of grass, with side entrance, lined with pieces of palm fronds and other plants. 3–8 whitish eggs, incubated by both sexes for 13–14 days; young, cared for by both parents, fledge in 25–28 days.

LIFESTYLE: With its essentially seed-based diet, strikingly patterned plumage and lively song, the Java sparrow is one of the most popular of all cagebirds. While this ensures its survival in captivity, it has meant that the species has become quite scarce in many parts of its native range, as wild birds have been caught to supply the demands of the international cagebird trade. It has also been extensively trapped in Indonesia for food. Furthermore, the Java sparrow has also been killed as a pest by farmers in rice-growing countries, owing to its fondness for this crop: at harvest time, huge flocks of Java sparrows can invade the rice paddies. Indeed, it is sometimes called "the ricebird" and its Latin name also reflects its feeding preferences, too, *Padda* referring to the rice-fields, or paddies, and *oryzivora* meaning "rice-eating."

FAITHFUL PARTNERS
Males and females have the same plumage, but females may have slightly smaller bills. They form exclusive pairs, probably for life. Males display to females by jumping up and down.

HOUSE SPARROW

Passer domesticus
Family: PLOCEIDAE
Order: PASSERIFORMES

DISTRIBUTION: Originally in open countryside and farmland from Europe and North Africa to western Asia. Has spread east across Asia to eastern Siberia, and south to Arabia and Myanmar (Burma). Introduced, and now naturally spreading, in North America, sub-Saharan Africa, and Australasia.

SIZE: Length 5.5–7in (14–18cm); weight 0.7–1.2oz (20–34g).

APPEARANCE: Small, short-legged, dumpy bird with stout, conical bill. Summer male has rich brown upperparts streaked with black; gray crown, white cheeks, and black eyestripe, chin and bib; blackish-brown primaries and tail feathers with pale edges; narrow white wingbar; grayish-white underparts. Bill black in summer, yellowish-brown in winter, when plumage is a duller brown. Female paler, more yellow-brown, with no black bib or eyestripe. Pale brown legs; light brown eyes.

DIET: Seeds, fruits, buds, flowers, insects, worms, and scraps.

BREEDING: Mainly in spring and summer. Pair build untidy globe-shaped nest of grasses, dry stems, and debris, lined with feathers, with side entrance; in tree, inside other nest, in wall crevice, or building. 3–6 whitish or bluish-white eggs, marked with shades of gray and brown, incubated mainly by female for 9–18 days. Chicks fledge at 11–18 days.

REGULAR BATH
House sparrows often bathe in water, then follow up with a "dust bath." The dust may soak up excess oil, and discourage blood-sucking parasites such as fleas and bird lice.

LIFESTYLE: The house sparrow is one of the most familiar small birds, and for good reason. It has learned to live alongside people and exploit the environments we create, and has followed us over much of the globe – sometimes with a little help, but mostly under its own power. In North America it was virtually unknown before the 19th century, but after being introduced to New York City in 1850 it spread across the continent in less than 50 years.

In country areas house sparrows feed mainly on grain, but in towns they make the most of backyard bird feeders, eating seeds, nuts and all kinds of kitchen scraps. They have learned to find food in the most unlikely places, including inside factory buildings and even down mineshafts. In summer some make a specialty of picking dead insects from auto grilles.

House sparrows are equally enterprising in their nesting habits, and have been found raising broods of young inside occupied buildings and even in vehicles left parked for long periods. They usually breed in stable colonies, with each pair staying together for life – although a high mortality rate often forces surviving partners to find new mates. House sparrows can also be promiscuous, and both sexes often mate with other partners.

HILL MYNAH

Gracula religiosa
Family: STURNIDAE
Order: PASSERIFORMES

DISTRIBUTION: Tropical forests up to 5,000ft (1,500m) in India, Sri Lanka, and Southeast Asia, excluding Philippines.

SIZE: Length 11.5in (29cm); weight 4.6–5.3oz (130–150g).

APPEARANCE: Medium-sized bird with chunky head and large, stout, orange bill. Mainly black, with glossy purple and green sheen; broad white band on primaries. Orange-yellow bare skin and fleshy wattles on sides of head and nape. Dark brown eyes; yellow legs.

DIET: Fruit (especially figs) and berries, buds, nectar; also insects and small lizards.

BREEDING: April to July. Makes loose nest of twigs, grass, debris and feathers in tree hole, up to 50ft (15m) above ground. 2 pale grayish or greenish eggs, marked with brown, incubated by both parents for 11–18 days. Chicks cared for by both parents.

LIFESTYLE: Famous for its skill as a mimic when kept as a pet, the hill mynah is a relative of the starlings that lives wild in the mountain forests of southern Asia. It often travels through the treetops in small temporary flocks foraging for food. Figs are a favorite, and it also tackles other fruits with large stones; it can devour a number of these in rapid succession, then regurgitate the stones later – helping to spread the seeds of the trees that it harvests. It also takes nectar, and often emerges from a flower with a dusting of pollen on its head. Since it frequently moves straight to another flower of the same type, it may have an important role as a plant pollinator.

As they feed, the birds call to each other with a mixture of whistles, warbles, and shrieks; they are particularly noisy when they leave their overnight roosts in the morning, and return to them

RELUCTANT MIMIC
Despite being the finest of all mimics, the hill mynah never imitates other bird species in the wild – although it mimics other mynahs.

at night. They fly from tree to tree with a switchback, undulating flight rather like that of a woodpecker. Once mated, hill mynah pairs stay together for life, feeding and roosting together as well nesting and rearing their young. They nest in tree holes, but unusually for hole nesters their eggs are blotched for camouflage, suggesting that they once used open nests. In some areas such as Assam special nest boxes are erected so that the chicks can be gathered for the pet trade – but despite this the hill mynah is still a common bird over most of its range.

SUPERB BIRD OF PARADISE

Lophorina superba
Family: PARADISAEIDAE
Order: PASSERIFORMES

DISTRIBUTION: Rainforest in mountains of New Guinea, at 5,000–7,300 feet (1,500–2,225m).

SIZE: Length 10in (25cm); weight 2.1–3.5oz (60–100g).

APPEARANCE: Male has jet-black plumage, with iridescent turquoise-blue crown and erectile breast shield that has a purple to purplish-red sheen when light falls on it at certain angles; elongated nape feathers, velvety black with a dark green iridescence, form a huge, erectile cape; bill black, legs blackish; eyes dark brown. Female has blackish-brown head and dark reddish-brown upperparts; underparts whitish, tinged rufous-brown on breast, finely mottled with grayish-brown to black.

DIET: Mainly fruits and berries; also seeds, insects, frogs, lizards.

BREEDING: Any month of the year; varies across range of species. Female builds bulky nest of twigs in tree (often in crown of a palm tree or tree fern), generally a few yards (or metres) above ground. 1–2 cream or buff eggs, spotted, blotched or streaked with brown, reddish-brown, bluish-gray or lavender, incubated by female alone probably for about 18–19 days (data obtained from captive birds only). Chicks may fledge at 17–30 days.

LIFESTYLE: Both male and female superb birds of paradise lead an essentially solitary life, though they may join other species of birds when foraging. The males spend most of their time high in the trees, while females and younger males (which share the female's duller plumage) spend far more time in the understory. It is likely that the sexes rarely meet except for the purpose of mating. Males display alone on high perches and on the ground, adopting extraordinary postures that show off their ornate

SHOWING OFF
This displaying male
extends his iridescent
turquoise and violet breast
shield, flicks his huge black
nape cape over his head,
and opens his bill to show
off a vivid yellow mouth.

plumage to full advantage. Each
male mates, or tries to mate, with
several females. Despite full legal
protection, many of the world's
42 species of birds of paradise are,
or are soon likely to be, threatened,
due mainly to the accelerating
destruction of their forest habitat.
The superb bird of paradise is one
of the more fortunate species, still
relatively common through almost
all of the upland forests of New
Guinea. A major reason for its
success is that it is an adaptable
species that is more tolerant of
fragmented and disturbed habitats.

219

SPOTTED BOWERBIRD

> *Chlamydera maculata*
> Family: PTILONORHYNCHIDAE
> Order: PASSERIFORMES

DISTRIBUTION: Dry, open, grassy woodlands and scrub; visits large gardens, orchards, vineyards; in central and eastern Australia, from south-west New South Wales (rare) to central Queensland coast.

SIZE: Length 10–12in (25–31cm); weight 4.6–5.5oz (130–155g).

APPEARANCE: A sturdy perching bird with a thick, slightly downcurved bill. Forehead to nape buff-brown, tinged silvery gray; male has vivid iridescent lilac-pink neck frill (reduced or absent in female), that is erected like an inverted fan when displaying; gray band on lower nape; upperparts brownish or blackish, with buff to orange-buff tips to feathers, giving spotted pattern; underparts cream-buff with grayish mottling and bars; tail dark brown with buff or whitish tips; legs brownish; bill black, inside of mouth yellow; eyes brown.

DIET: Mainly fruit, but also seeds, nectar, insects and spiders.

BREEDING: From August to March. Female makes shallow nest of sticks and twigs, thinly lined with small twigs and grass, in fork of tree among foliage or in clump of mistletoe. Usually 2, sometimes 1 or 3, pale greenish eggs with pale grayish-mauve blotches and dark brown scribbles, incubated by female for probably

FOOTLOOSE MALE
The male plays no part in nest-building, incubation or rearing the young. This species occurs solitarily, and in small flocks in winter, feeding at all levels from the ground to the tree canopy.

12–15 days. Chicks cared for by female; fledge at about 20-21 days.

LIFESTYLE: Like other bowerbirds, the male attracts several females to mate with him not by showing off extravagant plumage, but by enticing them to visit a large, structure, known as a "bower," which he builds for the purpose. That of the spotted bowerbird is an avenue, with two U-shaped walls and a floor of twigs lined with grass stems. He decorates this with hundreds of ornaments, such as bleached rabbit and sheep bones, white snail shells and pebbles, and glass of various hues, as well as stolen items, including cutlery, jewellery, coils, automobile keys, and even a glass eye in one recorded instance. The male displays to females that visit the bower, erecting his vivid neck frill, performing a stiff-legged dance, brandishing ornaments in his bill. As well as making hissing, grinding and clicking sounds he is a superb mimic, imitating the calls of many other birds, from whistling kites to butcherbirds; and many other sounds, including dog barking, whip-cracks and wood chopping.

SPOTTED NUTCRACKER

> *Nucifraga caryocatactes*
> Family: CORVIDAE
> Order: PASSERIFORMES

DISTRIBUTION: Coniferous and mixed forests of northern and mountainous regions of Eurasia, from Scandinavia east to Japan.

SIZE: Length 12.5–13.4in (32–34cm); weight 4.4–7oz (124–200g).

APPEARANCE: Pigeon-sized, with powerful, long, pointed bill, broad wings and short tail. Head and body plumage dark brown, peppered with big white spots except on crown and nape (southern races have fewer, smaller spots chiefly on face, upper back and breast only); wings black; sides of black tail and undertail white, and conspicuous in flight; bill and legs black, eyes dark brown.

DIET: Mainly seeds, specially of pines, nuts (hazel nuts); also insects and other invertebrates in summer and berries in autumn.

BREEDING: From mid-March. Nest a cup of twigs, bramble shoots and lichens with some mud and soil mixed in, lined with grass and other soft plant materials, typically about 20 feet (6m) high, sited on side branches against a conifer trunk. 2–5 pale blue or bluish-green eggs, finely marked with pale brown, incubated by both sexes for 16–18 days. Chicks cared for by both parents. Fledge at 21–28 days, but are not independent for a further 3 months or more.

LIFESTYLE: The spotted nutcracker hoards thousands of seeds and nuts to see it through winter. Most nutcrackers, which pair for life, stay where they are year-round, each pair defending their many hidden seed caches from rivals. They have an amazing memory for finding their stores, though they fail to eat all of them and so are vital in seeding forests.

Occasionally, large numbers of the thick-billed Siberian race are forced to leave their native forests by food shortages following failure of conifer seed crops, and "irrupt" far and wide into areas, including western Europe, that lie far from their normal range.

FRUIT AS A SUBSTITUTE
During their sporadic "irruptions," nutcrackers disperse widely, and eat a much wider range of food than in their native forests. This includes cultivated fruit such as apples.

Eurasian Jay

Garrulus glandarius
Family: CORVIDAE
Order: PASSERIFORMES

DISTRIBUTION: Woods and forests (especially of oaks but also other deciduous trees and conifers), parks and wooded gardens across Eurasia, from Europe and northwest Africa to Siberia, China, Japan, and parts of southeast Asia.

SIZE: Length 13in (33cm); weight 5–7oz (140–190g).

APPEARANCE: Medium-sized buffish to rufous or brownish-pink bird, with blackish-brown primary flight feathers and tail and bold white rump; the 33 or so different geographical races vary in plumage details; wings have black-barred bright blue patches and in most races white patches too; face varies from white to same color as body, with a variable black mustache stripe; in European and some other races the forehead and crown is paler with black streak, in others it is black or unmarked; some races have gray upper back; bill dark brown; eyes bluish-white, dark in some races.

DIET: Mainly nuts, seeds, fruits and berries, including many acorns in winter; also animal food, including large insects, small mammals, birds' eggs and nestlings, and carrion.

BREEDING: In spring and early summer. Pair build crude cup-shaped nest of twigs and stems, in small tree. 3–7 pale bluish, greenish or olive-buff eggs, densely speckled with brown, incubated for 16–19 days by female, who is fed by male. Chicks, fed by both parents, fledge at 18–23 days.

LIFESTYLE: One of the most beautiful of all members of the crow family, the Eurasian jay is generally shy and secretive, especially in Europe where it has long been persecuted for its depredations on gamebird eggs and chicks. In fact, it has a wide-ranging diet and does good by eating many caterpillars of moths that attack the leaves of trees. The jay also plays a vital role in the natural planting of oakwoods.

In autumn, the birds gather vast numbers of acorns to see them through the hard times of winter. They carry them, often far away, in a throat pouch to bury them in secret hoards. The birds only eat a proportion of their stores, and many of the abandoned acorns grow into new trees far from the parent trees. Oaks have probably evolved the tough, food-rich acorn specifically to attract the jays.

FAR-CARRYING CALL
The Eurasian jay's harsh, screeching "skaaak, skaaak" alarm call is a familiar sound of the oak woodlands.

ROCK DOVE

Columbia livia
Family: COLUMBIDAE
Order: COLUMBIFORMES

DISTRIBUTION: Original wild form on rocky cliffs and mountains across southern Eurasia from North Africa, western and southern Europe, through Arabia and Asia Minor to the Indian subcontinent. Feral form mainly in towns and cities, virtually worldwide.

SIZE: Length 12–13in (31–34cm); weight 8.8–12.3oz (250–350g).

APPEARANCE: Plump-bodied bird with short neck, small head, and short bill with fleshy "cere" at base around nostrils. Wild form bluish-gray with paler wings and back; iridescent green and purple gloss at sides of neck; wingtips darker with two black wing-bars; white rump visible in flight; black-tipped tail. Legs purplish-red; bill black, cere whitish. Feral "town pigeon" has similar form but thicker bill with large white cere, and very variable plumage.

DIET: Mainly seeds, grains, fruits, and other plant material; also snails, insects, and worms. Feral birds eat wide range of scraps.

BREEDING: Mainly in spring and summer, but often all year round, in colonies. Nest a sparse platform of twigs, stems, or roots. 2 white eggs, incubated by both parents for 17–19 days. Chicks fed at first on "pigeon milk," a curd-like substance secreted from lining of the crop and regurgitated. Chicks fledge at 30–35 days.

LIFESTYLE: Wild rock doves inhabit rocky, windswept cliffs and crags, in remote regions on coasts and inland, where they use their agility on the wing to swoop and glide on the turbulent updrafts around the rock faces. But between 5,000 and 10,000 years ago the rock dove became the first bird in history to be domesticated and reared for food.

Over time selective breeding produced over 350 different varieties of these domestic birds, and escapes from captivity over the years have created flourishing populations of "feral pigeons" that mostly live half-wild in cities. They have also interbred with the original wild birds, to the point where pure-bred rock doves are now rare, and found only in regions remote from pigeon-colonized cities. Meanwhile feral pigeons may become so numerous that they are culled by city authorities.

One odd feature of this bird is its ability to find its way home from great distances. Wild rock doves never stray far from their breeding sites, so this instinct is a mystery.

LOOKS FAMILIAR
The rather stout, dumpy form of the rock dove is familiar to anyone who lives in a city, since the common "town pigeon" is essentially the same bird.

SCARLET MACAW

Ara macao
Family: PSITTACIDAE
Order: PSITTACIFORMES

DISTRIBUTION: Lowland tropical forests and open woodlands from southern Mexico to northern Bolivia and central Brazil.

SIZE: Length 31.5–38in (80–96cm); weight 2–3.3lb (0.9–1.5kg).

APPEARANCE: Very large parrot with long, tapering tail. Color mainly scarlet; lower back, rump and tail coverts light blue; outer tail feathers blue; wing coverts yellow, tipped green; undertail pale blue: legs purplish-gray; upper mandible of bill pale horn color, lower mandible blackish; eyes pale yellow, surrounded by bare white face patch, which turns pinkish when the bird is excited.

DIET: Leaves, fruits, seeds, even sap; feeds high in trees.

BREEDING: Season varies with region; nests in cavities in trunks of tall dead trees. 2–4 white eggs, incubated by both parents for 24–25 days. Chicks fledge at 14 weeks.

LIFESTYLE: Scarlet macaws are very sociable birds, living in pairs, family groups or larger flocks of up to about 30 individuals. These brilliantly colored parrots make an unforgettable sight as they fly off at sunrise in search of food, their raucous screeching contact calls ringing through the forest. While feeding, though, they are usually silent. Scarlet macaws move about the forest to maintain a supply of food as the many different tree species from which they feed come into flower, fruit and seed in different places and at different seasons.

Their formidable bills can deal with large, hard seeds, but they also eat fruit and leaves. They also visit banks of clay, where they eat clay particles, probably to help them deal with toxic substances in some of the food they eat. At dusk, they return to their roosts high in the trees, which at times may contain as many as 50 birds.

The scarlet macaw is still relatively

common in the more remote parts of its extensive range, but in many places is severely threatened by logging and by trapping for the cagebird trade. It has suffered particularly drastic declines in Central America.

DEVOTED COUPLE

Like almost all parrots, scarlet macaws pair for life. A couple will stay close together all the time, both in the trees and in the air: they fly so close together that their wingtips almost touch.

KEA

NEW ZEALAND

Nestor notabilis
Family: PSITTACIDAE
Order: PSITTACIFORMES

DISTRIBUTION: Mainly around the tree-line at altitudes of 3,100–4,600 feet (950–1,400m) on the edge of wooded valleys and beech forests, in scrub and alpine grasslands, in the mountains of South Island, New Zealand. Tend to move uphill in fall and down to lower altitudes in winter.

SIZE: Length 18in (46cm); average weight 32.5oz (922g).

APPEARANCE: Large, heavily built parrot with long, pointed upper mandible (longest in male), sturdy legs and large feet. Dark brown head and underparts have darker tips to feathers, back and wings more strongly scaled with blacker edges to Iridescent bronzy-green feathers; wingtip feathers partly blue; underwings tangerine; tail bronze-green above, yellow below, dark band near tip; legs grayish-brown; bill black; eyes brown.

DIET: Mainly berries, shoots; also includes insects, carrion.

BREEDING: Mainly from July to January. Female makes nest of twigs, moss, lichens, leaves and chewed wood beneath rocks, under tree roots, or in hollow log. 2–4 white eggs, incubated by female for 23–24 days. Male brings food. Chicks cared for by both parents. Fledge at 13–14 weeks; become independent 4–6 weeks later.

LIFESTYLE: Like other parrots, keas are very social birds, often seen wheeling high above a forested valley on their broad wings, calling loudly. The call, a harsh, ringing "kee-ah", gave the bird its common name.

These are bold, playful, and inquisitive birds, supplementing their diet of natural foods, which include berries of many mountain shrubs and trees with food pilfered or scavenged from around ski-lodges, campsites and car-parks. Although they may seem abundant when they congregate at such places, there may be fewer than 5,000 of these lively birds left.

They sometimes cause damage to tents and cars, and until receiving legal protection in 1970, were killed in thousands by farmers who believed they killed sheep, though in fact it is now known that they rarely attack live animals.

MOUNTAINEER PARROT
Unlike most other parrots, the kea is at home high in the mountains, feeding among snow in alpine scrub and grasslands, reaching altitudes of up to 7,900ft (2,400m).

SULFUR-CRESTED COCKATOO

Cacatua galerita
Family: PSITTACIDAE
Order: PSITTACIFORMES

DISTRIBUTION: Woodland, forest, mangroves, grassland, farmland, parks, gardens in north and east Australia and offshore islands, New Guinea and offshore islands, and east Moluccan islands, Indonesia. Introduced to New Zealand.

SIZE: Length 18–22in (45–55cm); weight 29-34oz (815–975g).

APPEARANCE: Large parrot, with big powerful bill, short, rounded wings and tail, short legs and strong feet; almost entirely pure-white plumage, apart from very large, erectile, sulfur-yellow crest; tinge of yellow on cheek, and yellow wash on underwings and underside of tail; bill blackish, legs dark gray; eye very dark brown, with white (eastern Australian race), bluish (north-central Australian race) or blue (New Guinea and Indonesian race) ring around it.

DIET: Wide variety of seeds (including grains), fruits, and buds.

BREEDING: In Australia, from August to January in south and May to September in north; in New Guinea, in all months except April, but mainly from May to December. Nests in tree-hollow up to 100 feet (30m) above ground , lined with woodchips, more rarely in holes in cliffs. 2–3 white eggs, incubated by both parents for 25–27 days. Young fledge at about 6–9 weeks, continuing to roost in hollow for a further 2 weeks or more; fed by both parents. Remain with parents as part of local flock for several months. The only difference between male and female is that the male has a darker eye.

LIFESTYLE: These well-known birds are conspicuous as flocks gather at

CHARACTERISTIC FLIGHT
Sulfur-crested cockatoos are strong fliers, traveling considerable distances in search of food. They fly with bursts of stiff, shallow beats of their broad, rounded wings alternating with glides.

their roosts at sunset or leave them at dawn, uttering ear-splitting screeches and squawks. In the morning, they drink and fly to feeding areas. They rest in trees during the hottest part of the day.

Sulfur-crested cockatoos are often regarded as pests by farmers, as they eat ripening grain and grain fed to livestock.

During courtship, the male gives quiet, chattering calls, bobs and sways his head in a figure-of-eight pattern, and raises his crest.

Sulfur-crested cockatoos are extremely popular as cagebirds; overseas trade in wild-caught birds is illegal in Australia, and their populations there are stable. Many are still trapped in New Guinea, where they are also affected by clearance of forests.

BUDGERIGAR

Melopsittacus undulatus
Family: PSITTACIDAE
Order: PSITTACIFORMES

DISTRIBUTION: In the wild in wooded country, scrublands, grasslands, and cultivated land throughout Australia (excluding Tasmania), moving into coastal areas in spring and summer. Also kept as pets worldwide, but such birds are bred in captivity – trapping wild budgerigars is illegal.

SIZE: Length 6.5–7.8in (17–20cm); weight 29g (1oz).

APPEARANCE: Small parrot with long, pointed tail. Wild birds green with bright yellow crown, mask, and throat; black spots on throat; violet "mustache;" back barred with black. Pinkish-gray legs; grayish-yellow bill; base of bill and fleshy cere blue in male, brown in breeding female.

DIET: Seeds of grasses, herbs, and shrubs; also cereals.

BREEDING: Season varies with local rainfall. Many pairs nest close together, in holes in trees, fence posts, and logs. Eggs laid on layer of wood dust. 4–6 white eggs, incubated by female for 18 days; male stays nearby. Chicks are fed at first on a secretion from the female's crop, then on seeds. They fledge at 4 weeks, and remain with parents for a further 2 weeks.

LIFESTYLE: Budgerigars belong to a group of parrots called the "grass parakeets," which eat the seeds of grasses and other low-growing plants. They feed in flocks, moving over the ground in a broad wave and stripping every plant of its seeds by running the seedheads through their bills. The availability of seeds depends on the erratic rainfall of the Australian interior. The budgerigar flocks roam nomadically, following the rains and the seeds that appear in their wake. In poor seasons a local flush of food can attract flocks from a wide radius, which gather in vast aggregations of thousands of birds.

TRICK OF THE LIGHT
The green plumage is actually yellow, modified by a blue reflection from the feathers. If the yellow is removed by selective breeding, the bird looks blue.

Budgerigars breed at any time of year to make the most of periods when food is plentiful. They nest in loose colonies, using any suitable holes. Each female sits tight on her eggs while the male keeps her supplied with food, and when her eggs hatch she feed the nestlings on the protein-rich "crop milk" that oozes from her upper digestive tract. Young budgerigars are able to breed from the age of six months.

COCKATIEL

Nymphicus hollandicus
Family: CACATUIDAE
Order: PSITTACIFORMES

DISTRIBUTION: Lives in the arid and semi-arid regions of inland Australia. Northern populations roam nomadically; southern birds migrate north for the winter.

SIZE: Length: 13in (32cm); weight: 3–3.5oz (80–100g)

APPEARANCE: Slim, parrotlike bird with large head, hooked bill, and upward-pointing crest; long wings and tail. Mainly gray, with large white wing and shoulder patches. Pale yellow face, with gray patches and orange-red cheek spot; face colors more intense on male.

DIET: Small seeds, gathered from near the ground.

BREEDING: In August–December, in tree hole near water. Makes a soft platform of wood dust within the hole. Usually 5 white eggs; incubation 18–20 days, by both sexes; young fly at 4–5 weeks. May raise several broods, depending on local food supply.

LIFESTYLE: Familiar all over the world as a cage bird, the cockatiel is a small cockatoo that lives on the dry grasslands of Australia – a habitat that it shares with the equally familiar budgerigar. It has the same diet of small seeds, favoring those of grasses which are easy to gather from the ground. Seeding is unpredictable in the drought-prone Australian climate, so over much of its range the cockatiel is forced to live as a nomad, following the rains to find seeding crops of grass and other plants. Outside the breeding season it travels in small flocks of up to 30 or so, but many flocks may converge on a good feeding site. This can be a problem in areas where farmers grow seed crops such as sorghum or sunflowers, and the Australian government permits the shooting of cockatiels under license. This makes little impact on the total population, however, as cockatiels are able to make the most of any local glut of food to raise several broods of young, and they soon build up their numbers again. The spread of arable farming has also helped the cockatiel expand its range into once-barren areas of Australia where wild seeds are scarce.

REGULAR ROUTINE
Although they are nomadic opportunists, cockatiels always stick to the same daily routine. They feed only at sunrise and just before sunset, and spend much of their day resting.

EURASIAN CUCKOO

Cuculus canorus
Family: CUCULIDAE
Order: CUCULIFORMES

DISTRIBUTION: Breeds in wide variety of habitats with exception of desert and tundra, throughout Europe and Scandinavia, south to Morocco and Turkey, and east through much of northern Asia to eastern Siberia and China. Western birds winter in Africa south of the equator; eastern birds winter in Southeast Asia.

SIZE: Length 12.5–13.5in (32–34cm); weight 3.7–4.6oz (105–130g).

APPEARANCE: Falcon-like bird with small tapered head, long pointed wings, and long tail. Gray above, with darker tail; paler below with fine bars on breast, belly, and underwing. Male has dark chest, female has paler, brownish, barred chest. Some females are red-brown above with dark bars. Yellow legs; yellow, black-tipped bill.

DIET: Mainly caterpillars, including hairy varieties that other birds cannot eat; also other insects.

BREEDING: In spring, each female lays 1–25 eggs singly in the nests of songbirds such as warblers. Incubation 11–12 days, by hosts. Each chick destroys original brood of host; leaves nest at 17 days, and fledges at 17–21 days.

LIFESTYLE: The far-carrying two-note call of the male Eurasian cuckoo is welcomed throughout much of its northern range as a symbol of spring. But small birds have reason to fear the call if they could understand the implications, for like the American cowbirds the cuckoo is a notorious brood parasite. Instead of raising its own young, the female places each egg in the nest of another small bird. When the young cuckoo hatches, it ejects the other eggs from the nest, despite being naked and blind, so it can monopolize the food brought by the "host" birds. Eventually it outgrows the nest – and its hosts – so that they have to

feed it on the perch. They may keep this up for six weeks, but eventually the young cuckoo flies off, following the adults to the tropics for the winter.

The cuckoo has an unusual taste for the large, hairy caterpillars that most birds find inedible. The hairs are an irritant, but cuckoos are adapted to deal with them with a protective stomach lining that can be shed and renewed.

BROOD PARASITE
The cuckoo finds a suitable host nest, removes the egg (often eating it) and substitutes her own with similar markings.

HOATZIN

Opisthocomus hoazin
Family: OPISTHOCOMIDAE
Order: CUCULIFORMES

DISTRIBUTION: Wet forests of South America, from Guyana and Ecuador to Brazil, Bolivia, and the Orinoco and Amazon river basins.

SIZE: Length 23.5in (60cm); weight 1.9lb (855g).

APPEARANCE: Large, clumsy bird with heavy body, big tail, long neck and small head with large, spiky, reddish-brown crest. Upperparts dark brown, streaked with white on neck and shoulders. Outer flight feathers reddish; tail tipped with yellow. Blue bare skin on face; red eyes; dark legs; horn-colored bill.

DIET: Leaves of arum, legume trees, and other swamp plants.

BREEDING: Breeds in family groups in tropical rainy season, with up to 6 adults building nest and caring for eggs and young. Nest a frail platform of sticks in a tree above water. 2–5 yellowish-buff to creamy-white eggs, spotted with blue-violet or brown, incubated for

about 28 days. Young soon leave nest, but are fed by adults. If danger threatens, they may drop into the water.

LIFESTYLE: The ungainly, odd-looking hoatzin was once thought to be a primitive, living relative of the long-extinct archaeopteryx – a survivor from the earliest phase of bird evolution. But it is now seen as a highly specialized bird, superbly adapted to its unique way of life. It feeds almost exclusively on leaves, which are easy to find but difficult to digest. It has a huge muscular crop with horny ridges for grinding the leaves to a pulp, and bacteria in its gut that convert the plant fiber into sugars. The process produces a lot of smelly gas, and in Guyana it is known as the "stinking pheasant."

RELUCTANT FLIER
The hoatzin has only small flight muscles, but since it can find all the food it needs within a small area, it does not need to fly well and prefers to glide.

Hoatzins feed in the early morning and evening, for about four hours a day. They forage in family groups during the breeding season, but at other times they often feed in flocks of 40 or more, staying in contact with hoarse, croaking cries. Hoatzins breed in monogamous pairs, but are helped by their young from previous years. All the adults help incubate the eggs and raise the young, feeding them on a regurgitated mash of half-digested leaves. The young birds leave the nest soon after hatching, and are quite able to look after themselves. They have prehistoric-looking claws on their wings that help them scramble among the branches, and if they are attacked they dive into the water, swim to the shore and climb back up into the trees.

RUBY-THROATED HUMMINGBIRD

> *Archilochus colubris*
> Family: TROCHILIDAE
> Order: APODIFORMES

DISTRIBUTION: Breeds in eastern North America, from north of the Great Lakes to the Gulf of Mexico. Winters from Florida, Cuba, and Jamaica to Mexico and south to Cost Rica.

SIZE: Length: 3.75in (9.5cm); weight: 0.1oz (3g).

APPEARANCE: Minute, needle-billed bird, with small head, thin neck, pointed wings typical of hummingbirds, and spiky tail. Plumage mainly iridescent green, with whitish underparts; male has red throat. Black eyes and bill.

DIET: Nectar, tree sap, and small insects.

BREEDING: Spring to summer. Builds cup nest of bud scales, lichen, and spider silk, lined with plant down, on near-horizontal branch of tree in deciduous or mixed woodland. 2 white eggs, incubated by female for 16 days; young fledge at 15–20 days.

LIFESTYLE: The little ruby-throated hummingbird is one of the few hummingbirds to breed outside the warm tropics and subtropics of South and Central America. It regularly nests as far north as New Brunswick and Nova Scotia, where it has a problem getting enough nectar to eat when it arrives in spring. It makes up the shortfall with sugary tree sap, which it finds by searching the trees for feeding holes drilled by the yellow-bellied sapsucker – a type of woodpecker.

It also eats a lot of insects, which it normally captures during short aerial chases. But like all hummingbirds its main food is nectar, which it usually gathers from red and orange flowers such as columbine, trumpet creeper, bee-balm, and jewelweed. It finds plenty to eat in summer – and plenty to feed its young – but in the fall it is forced to migrate south to Central America. It may travel up to 3,500 miles (6,000km).

This is an immense journey that often includes an astonishing 620-mile (1,000-km) non-stop flight across the Gulf of Mexico – a prodigious feat for such a tiny bird. To achieve it, the ruby-throat has to eat enough to double its body weight before attempting the crossing, or it will not have enough energy reserves to make the flight.

NO ARTIFICIAL SWEETENERS
The female ruby-throated hummingbird has sole responsibility for raising her young, which she feeds on a regurgitated mixture of protein-rich insects and high-energy nectar.

RESPLENDENT QUETZAL

Pharomachrus mocinno
Family: TROGONIDAE
Order: TROGONIFORMES

DISTRIBUTION: Breeds in cloud forests in mountains of southern Mexico, Guatemala, Honduras, El Salvador, Nicaragua, Costa Rica, western Panama. May move lower down after breeding.

SIZE: Length 14–16in (36–40cm), with tail streamers measuring up to 25.5in (65cm) or more in males; weight 6.3–7.4oz (180–210g).

APPEARANCE: Medium-sized bird with large head, short, thick bill, big eyes, sturdy body, short legs and feet with two toes forward and two backward; male's upperparts, spiky head-crest, throat and upper breast, and long wing coverts and very long four narrow, flexible uppertail coverts brilliant iridescent green, appearing bright blue from some angles; flight feathers blackish, lower underparts bright red, undertail white. Female duller, with bronzy head, mainly green upperparts and largely gray underparts; bill yellow in male, blackish in female; legs grayish.

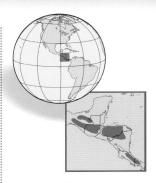

DIET: Mainly fruit, also some insects and other small animals such as snails, lizards and frogs.

BREEDING: March–June. Nest, without lining, inside a deep cavity 13–88 feet (4–27 m) high in the decaying wood of a tree or tree-stump. 1 or 2 eggs, incubated by both sexes for 17–19 days; young fledge in 23–31 days.

LIFESTYLE: With his stunning, greatly elongated, electric green display plumes, the male resplendent quetzal is justly regarded as one of the world's most beautiful birds. The name "quetzal" (pronounced "ketsaal") comes from the language of the Aztec people of Mexico. They revered male resplendent quetzals

FITTING IN
A male prepares to enter the nest hole to relieve his mate incubating the eggs within. It was once thought that he had to face away from the entrance so that his long tail covert feathers protruded out of the hole. In fact, they are so flexible that he can bend them double to protrude from the nest hole while he faces outward.

as sacred and trapped them to obtain their long feathers for use in headdresses by their rulers and priests. Anyone who killed the birds was punished by the death penalty. Today, after surviving hunting for the plume trade and more recently for zoos and private aviaries, resplendent quetzals are vulnerable to the destruction of the cloud forests, partly for growing coffee, and also to the lower forests.

TOCO TOUCAN

> *Ramphastos toco*
> Family: RAMPHASTIDAE
> Order: PICIFORMES

DISTRIBUTION: Forest edges, wooded savanna and plantations of eastern South America, from Guyana to northern Argentina.

SIZE: Length 21.5–24in (55–61cm); weight 1.1–1.9lb (500–860g).

APPEARANCE: Large bird with huge, deep bill up to 8.5 inches (21.5cm) long and short, rounded wings. Its feet have a yoke-toed arrangement, with two toes facing forward and two backward, giving it a strong grip on branches. Plumage black, with white throat and uppertail coverts and red undertail coverts; legs blue to grayish; bill bright reddish orange with black band at base and large black patch at tip of upper mandible; eyes brown, surrounded by patch of orange bare skin.

DIET: Mainly fruits, birds' eggs and nestlings; also insects and spiders.

BREEDING: Season varies. Nests in tree holes, often abandoned by or stolen from other birds, lined with fruit stones. 2–4 white eggs, incubated by both parents for 17–18 days. Chicks cared for by both parents; fledge at 43–52 days.

LIFESTYLE: Like those of other toucans, the toco toucan's amazing bill is a hollow structure of light-weight horn supported by internal struts. It is a highly efficient, accurate food-gathering organ; using the tip of its bill, the bird can pick up a fruit with great dexterity and toss it into the back of its throat to swallow it – or pluck an unfortunate nestling bird from deep within a tree hole.

FRUIT PLUCKER
Its huge bill allows the toco toucan to reach fruit at the edges of trees. These would otherwise be denied it because the toucan is too heavy to perch on slender branches.

The enormous bill serves other functions, too. It can be used to threaten other kinds of birds competing for limited supplies of fruit, and to frighten off the parents of the nestlings that form part of the toucan's diet. Toucans also use the bill as a dueling weapon in dramatic bouts of bill-fencing, probably connected with establishing dominance within the group. Largest of all toucans, the toco is usually seen in small flocks of up to 12 birds. They live in the trees, perching and feeding high in the canopy, but sometimes descend to the ground where they move with big hops. Toucans are noisy birds, frequently uttering deep, grunting, honking calls. In flight they also display a weak flap-and-glide action, in which they gradually lose height.

RHINOCEROS HORNBILL

> *Buceros rhinoceros*
> Family: BUCEROTIDAE
> Order: PICIFORMES

DISTRIBUTION: Forests of lowlands and foothills in extreme southern Thailand, Malaysian peninsula, Sumatra, Java and Borneo.

SIZE: Length 31–35in (80–90cm); weight, males 5.5–6.6lb (2.5–3kg), females 4.4–5.1lb (2–2.3kg).

FORM: Large bird with broad wings, long tail and very large down-curving bill topped by bony casque. Front 3 toes webbed at base. Plumage mainly black (with green gloss in male) apart from white thighs and undertail; tail white with broad black band; legs olive green; bill and casque ivory to pale yellow, often stained orange-red with preen oil; males have red eyes, with surrounding bare skin black; females have white eyes with an orange surrounding ring.

DIET: Mainly fruits, especially figs of many species; also small animals, chiefly large insects but also tree frogs and lizards; also birds' eggs.

BREEDING: Nests in tree holes. Female seals herself inside for defense against predators using mainly her own droppings, leaving small hole for bill to protrude. 1–2 white eggs, incubated by female for 37–46 days; male feeds her and chicks, then after about 3 months in nest, female breaks free; chicks reseal hole and both parents feed young, which fledge at 78–80 days.

LIFESTYLE: This impressive bird usually forages in pairs, though small flocks may gather at fruiting trees outside the breeding season.

The rhinoceros hornbill plucks fruit deftly from trees with its immense bill, manipulating the food delicately in the tip. It can break or crush larger items and discard inedible parts such as fruit husks or insect wings. Finally, it tosses the food into its throat with amazing accuracy. The bill, casque, and white parts of the plumage are often stained with its orange-red

preen oil. It collects this by wiping its bill on the preen gland at the base of its tail and then applies it to its plumage before cleaning it.

The function of the big, upcurved casque atop the bill (a structure unique to hornbills) may be to serve as a social or sexual signal, or to amplify calls. The rhinoceros hornbill has an extraordinary roaring call. Also, its wings make a very loud whooshing noise when it flies. These are among the most characteristic sounds of the forest where this magnificent bird still

GOOD PROVIDER
Contrary to popular belief, the male hornbill does not force his mate to imprison herself in the nest cavity. Indeed, he keeps her alive by making sure he brings her food.

occurs, though logging is reducing numbers in many places, and the bird is also hunted for food, the cagebird trade and for its bill and tail feathers, which are used in the ceremonies of indigenous peoples.

GLOSSARY

ADAPTATION features of an animal that adjust it to its environment; may be produced by evolution, e.g., camouflage coloration.

ADULT a fully grown sexually mature animal; bird in final plumage.

ALGAE primitive plants or plantlike organisms, ranging from microscopic forms to big seaweeds.

ALPINE living in mountainous areas, over 5,000 feet (1,500m).

ARBOREAL living in trees.

ARTHROPOD member of the largest phylum in the animal kingdom, having a hard, jointed exoskeleton and paired jointed legs. Includes insects, spiders, crabs, etc.

BILL often called the beak: the jaws of a bird, consisting of two bony **MANDIBLES**, upper and lower, and their horny sheaths.

BIODIVERSITY the variety of species and **ECOSYSTEMS** in the world and variation between them.

BIOME major world landscape with similar plants and animals living in it, e.g., desert, jungle, forest.

BIPED animal walking on two legs.

BREEDING SEASON the entire cycle of reproductive activity, from courtship, pair formation through nesting to independence of young.

BROOD young hatching from a single **CLUTCH** of eggs.

CAGE BIRD A bird kept in captivity, including birds taken from the wild.

CANOPY continuous (closed) or broken (open) upper layer in forests produced by the intermingling of branches of trees.

CARNIVORE meat-eating animal.

CARPAL the outer joint of the wing, the equivalent of the human wrist.

CARRION rotting flesh of dead animals.

CASQUE a bony extension of the upper **MANDIBLE**.

CLASS a large group of related animals. Mammals, birds, and reptiles are all classes of animals.

CLOUD FOREST moist, high-altitude forest characterized by a dense understory and an abundance of other plants growing on the trunks and branches of trees.

CLUTCH set of eggs laid by bird in a single breeding attempt.

COLONIAL living together.

CONIFEROUS FOREST evergreen forests found in northern regions and mountainous areas, dominated by pines, spruce, and cedars.

COVERTS feathers on a bird that overlap at least the bases of other feathers: wing coverts partly cover the flight feathers, tail coverts overlie the tail feathers.

CROP thin-walled extension of a bird's gullet, used for food storage (often to take food to the nest).

CRUSTACEAN member of a class in the phylum Arthropoda typified by five pairs of legs, two pairs of antennae, a joined head and thorax, and calcareous deposits in the exoskeleton, e.g., crabs.

DECIDUOUS FOREST dominated by trees that lose their leaves in winter (or in the dry season).

DEFORESTATION the process of cutting down and removing trees for timber or to create open space for growing crops, grazing animals.

DESERT area of low rainfall typically with sparse vegetation or lacking it altogether.

DISPERSAL scattering of young animals to live away from where they were born and raised.

DIURNAL active during the day.

DOMESTICATION process of taming and breeding animals to provide help and products for humans.

ECOLOGY the study of plants and animals in relation to one another and to their surroundings.

ECOSYSTEM a whole system in which plants, animals, and their environment interact.

ENDEMIC found only in one geographical area, nowhere else.

EXTINCTION process of dying out at the end of which the very last individual dies, and the species is lost forever.

FAMILY a group of closely related species that often also look quite similar. Zoological family names always end in -idae. Also used to describe a social group of parents and their offspring within a species.

FLEDGING PERIOD the time taken for a young bird to fledge, i.e. acquire its first full set of feathers, by the end of which it is (unless a flightless species) ready to fly.

FLEDGLING a young bird that has just fledged.

GAMEBIRD birds in the order Galliformes (grouse, turkeys, partridges, pheasants and relatives); also any birds that may be legally hunted by humans.

GENUS (genera, pl.) a group of closely related species.

HEN any female bird.

HERBIVORE animal that feeds on plants.

INCUBATION the act of keeping the egg or eggs warm or the period from the laying of eggs to hatching.

INDIGENOUS living naturally in a region; native (i.e. not an introduced species).

INSECT any air-breathing arthropod of the class Insecta, having a body divided into head, thorax, and abdomen, three pairs of legs, and sometimes two pairs of wings.

INSECTIVORE insect eater.

INVERTEBRATES animals that have no backbone (or other bones) inside their body, e.g. mollusks, insects, jellyfish, crabs.

IRIDESCENT displaying glossy colors; produced in bird **PLUMAGE** by splitting of sunlight into light of different wavelengths.

JUVENILE a young animal that has not yet reached breeding age; a young bird in its first proper covering of feathers that replace its baby down.

KERATIN the substance from which feathers are formed (also reptile scales, human hair, and fingernails).

MANDIBLE one of the jaws of a bird that make up the **BILL** (upper or lower).

MIGRATION movement from one place to another and back again; usually seasonal.

MOLT Shedding of old, worn feathers and replacement by new ones, at least once a year.

MONTANE a mountain environment.

NATURAL SELECTION the main process driving evolution in which animals and plants are challenged by natural effects (such as predators and bad weather), resulting in survival of the fittest.

NESTLING a young bird still in the nest and dependent on its parents.

NOCTURNAL active at night.

NOMADIC animals that have no fixed home, but wander about.

OMNIVORE an animal that eats a wide range of both animal and vegetable food.

ORDER a subdivision of a class of animals, consisting of a series of animal families.

ORGANISM any member of the animal or plant kingdom; a body that has life.

ORNITHOLOGIST zoologist specializing in the study of birds.

OVIPAROUS producing eggs that hatch outside the body of the mother (in fish, reptiles, birds, etc).

PAIR BOND the faithfulness of a mated pair to each other.

PARASITIZE referring to birds, usually to lay eggs in the nests of another species and leave the foster parents to raise the young. Birds that do this are called brood parasites.

PASSERINE often called "perching birds," although many others can perch; any bird of the order Passeriformes; includes songbirds.

PELAGIC living in the upper waters of the open sea or large lakes.

PHYLUM zoological term for a major grouping of animal classes. The animal kingdom is divided into about 30 phyla, of which the vertebrates form part of just one.

PLUMAGE the covering of feathers on a bird's body.

POPULATION a distinct group of animals of the same species or all the animals of that species.

PREDATOR an animal that kills live prey.

PRIMARY FEATHER one of the large feathers of the outer wing.

PRIMARY FOREST forest that has always been forest and has not been cut down and regrown at some time.

RACE see **SUBSPECIES**

RANGE the total geographical area over which a species is distributed.

RAPTOR a bird of prey, usually one belonging to the order Falconiformes.

REPTILE any member of the cold-blooded class Reptilia, such as crocodiles, lizards, snakes, with external covering of scales or horny plates.

ROOST place that a bird or bat regularly uses for sleeping; to sleep in such a place.

SAVANNA tropical grasslands with scattered trees and low rainfall.

SCRUB vegetation dominated by shrubs (woody plants usually with more than one stem).

SECONDARY FEATHER one of the large flight feathers on the inner wing.

SPAWNING the laying and fertilizing of eggs by fish, amphibians, etc.

STEPPE open grassland in parts of the world where the climate is too harsh for trees to grow.

SUBSPECIES a subpopulation of a single species whose members are similar to each other but differ from the typical form for that species; often called a race.

TAXONOMY the branch of biology concerned with classifying organisms into groups according to similarities in structure, origins, or behavior. The major categories, in order of increasing broadness, are: species, genus, family, order, class, phylum.

TERRESTRIAL living on land.

TERRITORY defended space.

TUNDRA open grassy or shrub-covered lands of the far north.

UNDERSTORY lower layer of trees and shrubs in a forest.

VERTEBRATE animal with a backbone, usually with skeleton made of bones, but sometimes softer cartilage.

WATTLE a fleshy protuberance, usually near the base of the bill.

WETLANDS fresh- or saltwater marshes.

ZOOLOGIST person who studies animals. (Zoology is the study of animals).

INDEX